Day Nurseries at a Crossroads

Meeting the challenge of child care in the nineties

Jeni Vernon and Celia Smith

The National Children's Bureau was established as a registered charity in 1963. Our purpose is to identify and promote the interests of all children and young people and to improve their status in a diverse society.

We work closely with professionals and policy makers to improve the lives of all children but especially young children, those affected by family instability, children with special needs or disabilities and those suffering the effects of poverty and deprivation.

We collect and disseminate information about children and promote good practice in children's services through research, policy and practice development, publications, seminars, training and an extensive library and information service.

The Bureau works in partnership with Children in Wales and Children in Scotland.

ISBN 1 874579 36 9

Published by the National Children's Bureau, 8 Wakley Street, London EC1V 7QE. Telephone 071 843 6000. Registered charity number 258825
Typeset by Books Unlimited (Nottm), Rainworth, Notts NG21 0JE
Printed by Biddles Ltd, Guildford

Contents

List of tables

List of figures

The authors

Jeni Vernon is a Senior Research Officer undertaking research consultancy projects on behalf of corporate members of the National Children's Bureau. She has been carrying out research in several aspects of children's services since the early seventies. She is co-author of **In Care: a study of social work decision making** (1986) and more recently has written reports on children with special educational needs, residential care and the organisation of services for children and families.

Celia Smith has worked in the field of child care in statutory and voluntary sectors since 1974. She has co-authored several books and reports including **A Family Support Model of Day Care: a study of pre-school projects in Barnardo's London Division** (National Children's Bureau, 1993) and **Confident Parents, Confident Children: policy and practice in parent education and support** (National Children's Bureau, 1994).

Foreword

In October 1989 we launched our Childcare Scheme with the opening of our first nursery in Sheffield. This step was hailed as a pioneering initiative on the part of a major employer to give serious consideration to the practical importance of child care. Now, some five years later, our scheme includes 115 nurseries and 60 holiday playschemes. We wholly own two of the nurseries ourselves but the remainder are run – as are the holiday playschemes – on a partnership basis, mainly with other public sector employers.

Although our child care policy is business driven, it has always been based on the principle that the first priority of any nursery is the quality of care it gives to its children. Partnership arrangements have enabled us to share the costs and risks of setting up nursery provision and mean that nurseries are based in the community, not the workplace, a feature much welcomed by parents.

Such is Midland's commitment to child care that the Bank is a founder member of Employers for Childcare, a forum which urges the government to take the lead in establishing a national child care policy through which accessible, affordable child care of quality will be available for all who require it.

In commissioning this work from the National Children's Bureau some two years ago, we were looking for an independent evaluation of the nursery provision we offer. We had no doubt, however, that the research would have implications extending well beyond ourselves. The publication of this book represents a landmark in our work on family friendly policies and we are delighted that it has come to fruition during this, the United Nations Year of the Family.

Anne Watts, O.B.E
Equal Opportunities Director
Midland Bank
August 1994

Acknowledgements

There can be little doubt that child care is an issue of growing public and professional interest in contemporary Britain and we should like to pay tribute to Midland Bank for the unique initiative they have displayed in commissioning this research. Anne Watts, the Bank's Equal Opportunities Director, has been involved in the research from the outset and, with Adele Kemmitt, Central Childcare Manager, has always been a source of encouragement. We would also like to express our gratitude to several colleagues in the Early Childhood Unit at the Bureau: although not actively involved in the research themselves Ann Robinson, Dorothy Rouse, Gillian Pugh and Liz Cowley have each given generously of their time and professional expertise. Other commitments meant that we were unable to undertake all the fieldwork ourselves and we are indebted to Janet Ames and Sue Finch who both stepped in temporarily to help us in this respect. We alone take responsibility for the report but would like to thank Ruth Sinclair, our Research Director, for tirelessly reading and commenting on drafts, and Sabina Collier for undertaking the lion's share of coordinating the manuscript.

Finally we would like to express our appreciation to the staff and parents of all the nurseries who participated in the research. Many nursery staff, we know, were anxious about our visits and we hope that they – and the parents – feel that their contribution has been worth while.

Jeni Vernon
Celia Smith
August 1994

Introduction

When the opportunity was presented by Midland Bank to undertake this research on day nurseries, we warmly welcomed it. As an organisation committed to children's interests and the promotion of their well-being, it was clearly relevant to our corporate agenda. Indeed the Early Childhood Unit at the Bureau, amongst others, has for some time now stressed the value to society at large of investing in services for young children (National Children's Bureau, 1990 and Holtermann, 1992). In addition, there have been relatively few studies of nurseries in this country – and those that have been carried out have tended to be small scale and limited in scope, or have focused on public sector nurseries with a highly selective group of children (Parry and Archer, 1974; Clark and Cheyne, 1979; Garland and White, 1980; Bain and Barnett, 1980; Clark and others, 1982; Van der Eyken, 1984 and Penn, 1991). The Bank's invitation, then, presented a unique opportunity to involve more than 100 nurseries, providing almost 4,000 places, in an assessment of group day care provision in the post Children Act era.

In Britain, the demand for provision for pre-school children – of which nurseries are but one part – has steadily risen as the number of women with young children entering the labour market continues to increase, sometimes on the basis of choice but often on the basis of economic necessity. Nonetheless, policy in this country persists in seeing children as the responsibility of their parents, not of society as a whole – and the role of the State as regulator, rather than provider. The structure of pre-school services in Britain which has resulted from this policy has been described by some as offering choice and diversity, by others as patchy and fragmented. Our own view is that nursery provision needs to be seen within the context of this overall framework and it is for this reason that we have devoted the opening chapter to a relatively brief summary of the main developments and issues around the broader theme of the care and education of young children.

Our second chapter deals more specifically with one of these issues, defining quality. For many years research in this country and abroad has tended to focus on whether or not non-parental day care was inherently bad for children and on the relative advantages and disadvantages for children of different forms of care. For a variety of reasons, it has rarely been possible to draw general conclusions from such research and more recent commentators have preferred to reformulate the issue as the need 'to identify conditions in each setting which may increase the risk of adverse effects or increase the potential for positive effects' (Moss and Melhuish, 1991). As these writers point out:

> Children are likely to benefit from an environment which provides a mixture of the best features from individual and group care. For example, good quality individual care can provide close attention to the individual needs of a child, while good quality group care can provide valuable social experience fostering social development: the balance needed between these qualities will vary between children, according to age, temperament and other factors. (p.131)

'Quality' has therefore become an important issue. However, arriving at an acceptable definition of 'quality' – and identifying measures of quality – has not always been a straightforward process. As the Guidance to the most recent legislation concerning day care for young children – the 1989 Children Act – acknowledges, a range of factors needs to be taken into account:

> Defining quality of care involves looking (at a range of factors) from the point of view of child development as well as the rights or expectations of children, parents and people working with young children. (Department of Health, 1991)

In chapter 2, then, we consider the issues around the theme of quality and describe our own approach to this matter in carrying out the research.

The next six chapters report the results from our research study. The data which form the basis of these chapters is drawn from a combination of a number of research techniques: survey, interview and observation undertaken over two phases. In the first phase, the 112 nurseries involved in a partnership agreement with Midland Bank in 1992 were asked to complete a questionnaire, the main purpose of which was to obtain a broad overview of current practice. The topics covered, then, included the management and philosophy of the nursery, hours of opening and the number of places offered, the admission procedure, the age range catered for, how children are grouped in the nursery, staffing and staff management and development, equal opportunities, premises, safety, health and hygiene, food and diet, programmes for children, monitoring children's learning and development, partnership with parents and links with other agencies. Ultimately, 85 per cent of the questionnaires were returned.

A second stage of the project entailed a more in-depth evaluation of 15 nurseries, these being selected on the basis that they were broadly representative of the group responding to the questionnaire. Each nursery was visited by a member of the research team for three to four days during the spring and summer of 1993. During this period, key personnel were interviewed, a parents' questionnaire was distributed and a small sample of parents who had employer-assisted provision were interviewed. However, the main purpose of this fieldwork was to observe nursery practice and we identified the following aspects as being particularly significant:

- whether and how children's development was encouraged – cognitively, physically, socially, emotionally and linguistically;
- whether and how staff encouraged and extended children's learning;
- whether and how children's self-esteem was promoted and children's identity respected by staff;
- the extent to which anti-discriminatory attitudes and practices were promoted and encouraged;
- how children were spending their time in the nursery, and how this was determined;
- how the nursery staff interacted with children, each other and with parents;
- how children interacted with one another;
- the amount of indoor and outdoor space and how the nursery made use of this;
- the range of play equipment available and how it was used by staff;
- whether and how children's development was monitored, assessed and recorded;
- the roles of individual staff members and whether and how a key worker system was in operation;
- the management of the nurseries, including parents' role;
- the routines and activities of the nursery.

In order to ensure comparability between the nurseries – and researchers – an objective measure of each nursery's 'performance' was clearly necessary. After considering a range of methods and instruments used by others, we decided that none entirely met our criteria and that selective use should be made of a number of approaches, each of which would complement and supplement the others. The methods and instruments ultimately adopted are discussed in greater detail in chapter 2.

Since there is clearly some overlap between the data from the two research phases, in presenting our findings, we have drawn selectively on these for different chapters. Drawing on the postal survey, then, chapter 3 paints a broad picture of the nurseries: where they are located, the number of children they deal with, the fees charged and so forth. Subsequent chapters utilise information from both phases of the research. Chapter 4 looks at the nurseries in relation to a range of policy, management and staffing issues and chapter 5 at the physical environment of the nurseries. In chapters 6 and 7, nursery practice is examined in terms of the service offered to children, whilst in chapter 8 we consider both parents' expectations of nursery placement and how the concept of 'working in partnership with parents' operates in practice. Finally, in chapter 9, we summarise the main findings of the research and consider their implications for the development of services to young children.

We hope that there is something in this book for the wide range of individuals now involved with day care, be that as parents, as practitioners and managers, as regulators or as policy makers. Above all, of course, we would like to think that the research will ultimately be of benefit to the child users of nursery provision. As one parent involved in the research put it:

> As a parent, you do have misgivings... I hope this report will provide guidelines to parents about those misgivings which are an acceptable part of life and those which are of greater importance to a child's security and future happiness.

1. Policy and provision: the changing context of early childhood day care services

Although the subject of this research is day nurseries, this particular provision cannot be viewed in isolation from developments in thinking, policy and provision in the field of pre-school services more generally. This chapter begins, then, with a brief description of the manner in which pre-school provision has developed in this country. We then turn to look more specifically at day care and discuss how, although national policy has remained largely unchanged, levels and types of day care provision have been influenced by a range of economic, ideological and social factors. Before concluding the chapter, the position in Britain is examined with reference to developments in the wider European Union.

Pre-school services in Britain

There has been a tradition in this country of dividing services for young children into two groups: day care and pre-school education. Pre-school education has generally been offered on a part-time basis to children over the age of three in nursery schools or in nursery classes attached to schools. In contrast, day care (also often referred to as 'child care') is much less easily defined – not least because the meaning attached to it has varied over time. Currently, however, few would disagree that day care is concerned with the care of pre-school aged children in a variety of non-school settings such as with relatives, childminders or in day nurseries. The values underlying each of these broad types of provision differ. In the case of pre-school education, recognition of the importance of early childhood development and its impact on subsequent educational achievement are fundamental considerations. In relation to day care, the situation is much less clear cut, but with day care having its origins in the need for non-parental care in parents' absence (for whatever reasons), the emphasis has been much less on a specifically educational input.

As Hennessy and others (1992) point out this division has affected both the services themselves and the research that has been carried out in relation to them. For example, research on pre-school education has tended to focus on the likely positive consequences for children of this type of experience and has carried considerable weight in a number of official reports (see, for example, Education Select Committee, 1989 and Department of Education and Science, 1990). Day care research, on the other hand, has tended to concentrate on more negative questions – in particular, is day care bad for children? Likewise, as the above authors have pointed out, we now have a situation in this country where there are major inconsistencies between day care and pre-school education in terms of funding, costs to parents, availability, hours of opening, administrative responsibility, the training and pay of workers and overall orientation. Whilst official sources tend to argue that this situation has led to choice and diversity, more commonly commentators have referred to the outcome as patchy and fragmented (Pugh, 1988 and 1992, and Penn and Riley, 1992). Certainly for parents seeking access to provision this situation can create a great deal of confusion.

In recent years there has been a growing recognition that 'care' and 'education' are inseparable when thinking of young children and the current division of services has been challenged on this basis. Indeed several organisations including the European Childcare Network (Cohen, 1988), the National Children's Bureau (1990), the Equal Opportunities Commission (1990), the National Consumer Council (1991) and the Association of Metropolitan Authorities (1991), have put forward radical proposals for change and called for a comprehensive national strategy. Whilst little progress has been made in this respect, there have been some other positive indicators of change.

Two of these changes are particularly relevant in this context. Cursory examination of one of these – the search for a more appropriate terminology – may appear at first sight trivial but has had – and seems likely to continue to have – an impact. As Moss (1992) has pointed out our limited English-language terminology both reflects and reinforces existing artificial divisions. Thus, whilst the term 'educare', introduced as an alternative conveying a more integrated approach, has gained little favour, the notion of early childhood services is now much more widely subscribed to. Although this development has had limited impact on the organisation of services, it has both begun to introduce a commonality of purpose across those working with young children and given increased recognition to the idea that the notion of 'curriculum' (describing all the experiences and activities that are offered to children) is as applicable to day care services as it is to pre-school education. In addition, recent legislation in the form of the 1989 Children Act has heralded change. Although the Act and its Guidance do not themselves use the term 'curriculum', there is a clear emphasis placed on the need for day care services to plan and support children's learning and development. Furthermore the Act **requires** education authorities and social services departments, to work together in relation to a number of aspects of the development of services. Given that the Act was not implemented until late in 1991, it is too early to assess its impact on practice. What is clear, however, is that the potential is there to radically reappraise services to young children.

Day care: policy and provision

There is widespread consensus that national policy in this country has rarely veered from the position that the care of young children is a predominantly private matter, with public involvement restricted to those specific instances where children's welfare and protection are at risk. Thus, the quantity and range of provision has been determined by a range of economic, ideological and social factors. For example during both World Wars, day nurseries were publicly provided in order to free women, in the national interest, to work in munitions factories and other industrial settings. With the removal of that stimulus and the subsequent influence of writers such as Bowlby (1952), the number of day nurseries in England and Wales had reduced within the space of 20 years to only one third of the number operating in 1945.

The reduction in public nursery provision had two significant consequences: first the public provision which did remain available became rationed. By 1968, then, the government was recommending that priority be accorded to providing places to children with only one parent 'who has no option but to go out to work' and broadly on health or welfare grounds relating to the child or mother (Ministry of Health, 1968). This trend has continued and there are now few publicly provided nurseries which offer an open-door facility: indeed public provision has increasingly become restricted to those children where social needs within the family place the child 'at risk'. Much public nursery provision has therefore taken on a 'welfare' role and, as such, using it tends to be stigmatising.

Secondly, the demand for day care clearly did not diminish in response to the contraction in public provision, the gap left being filled by a range of services offered by the independent and voluntary sectors. For example, childminders were first required to be registered by the 1948 Nurseries and Childminders Regulation Act and it is notable that between 1949 and 1968, the number of places with registered childminders in England and Wales increased from 1700 to 47,200. The playgroup movement has also been a development of post war Britain, playgroups tending to cater for children over three years. Traditionally they have offered children **and** parents opportunities for organised play activities on a part-time sessional basis and, as such, they have generally not been viewed as offering a day care service to parents. More recently, an increasing number of playgroups are available on an all-day basis.

Over the past 20 years, two further factors have combined to heighten demand for child care services. Thus, in the employment sector, pressure for equal opportunities for women has resulted in increasing numbers of women remaining in and returning to the labour market. Secondly, changes in the labour market itself are increasingly placing women's employment at a premium. Whilst the so-called 'demographic time bomb' – the drop in the number of young workers available to join the labour market in the early 1990s – may have been temporarily defused, the shift in the workforce from manufacturing to service industries is likely to be of longer term benefit to women workers. Thus, whilst women's participation in the labour market in the sense of full-time employment may not be as great in Britain as elsewhere, there are clear indications that women's return to work is now much less likely to be delayed till children go to school than once was the case. Indeed, Breeze and others (1991) have shown that whereas in 1973, 25 per cent of women whose youngest child was under five had paid employment and only seven per cent worked full-time, by 1989 the corresponding figures were 41 and 12 per cent. More recent figures suggest that this is a continuing trend with 49 per cent of women whose youngest dependent child is aged 0-4 years being economically active, almost

Figure 1.1 Total number of day care places, England 1983–1993

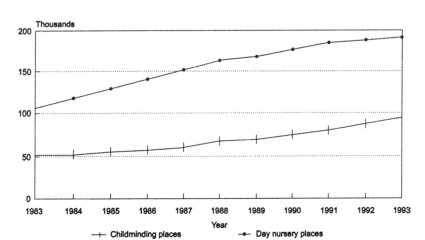

Source: Department of Health (1994) *Children's Day Care Facilities at 31.3.93*. Personal Social Services Local Authority Statistics.

14 per cent of these working full-time (source: Employment Department 1991 Labour Force Survey).

According to Marsh and McKay (1993), **most** day care continues to be provided by relatives and friends. However, they also report a steady increase in the use of 'professional' care, particularly for pre-school children. Almost half the working mothers with children under five use this type of care to some degree. Figure 1.1 shows the increase in the number of places available with childminders and in day nurseries over the past decade.

The manner in which national statistics are collected make it difficult to be precise about the growth in the size of the private nursery sector. However, the heightened demand for child care is most dramatically shown by the growth in the number of non-local authority nursery places becoming available. Thus, although between 1975 and 1985 there was only a limited increase in the number of such places, over the next eight years there was a fourfold increase, from 25,242 in 1985 to 111,000 in 1993.

Faced with the need to retain skilled female workers but a lack of public day care provision, employers have become more involved with child care issues, and with family friendly policies more generally (see for example, Business in the Community/Institute of Personnel Management, 1993). Over the past few years, then, a growing number of employers – but notably the larger companies – have increasingly been attempting to help staff combine work and family responsibilities. In consequence, a wide range of measures is gradually being introduced and developed to suit the needs of individual companies. The pattern is by no means uniform but flexible working practices are now more commonplace: job-sharing, career break schemes, extended maternity leave and parental leave. More specifically in relation to the care of children, some employers now assist employees with locating provision by using information services, such as Childcare Solutions, or locally based information services. Others provide some level of subsidy, in the form of vouchers such as Childcare Vouchers, or part payment of child care costs. Funding of 'childminding networks' has proved appropriate for some companies, whilst others have gone yet further and set up their own 'workplace' nurseries for the exclusive use of their employees: there are now estimated to be some 500 workplace nurseries in England and Wales.

However businesses have found that, of all the family friendly policies, child care has been the most problematic to set up and the most difficult to monitor. On account of this several employers have formed a Forum, **Employers for Childcare,** which calls on the government to develop a national framework which delivers 'accessible, available, affordable and quality childcare services'. The Forum's launch document states that the overall objective of such a strategy should be 'to enable more parents of children aged 0-14 years to participate in the labour market.' The Forum advocates a partnership between employers, government, parents, local agencies and providers, each of which can contribute from its own area of expertise – for employers, this would comprise funding, motivation and detailed experience. The members of the Forum call on the government to consider the following action:

- establishing a government working group with employers and relevant organisations to consider child care issues;
- the establishment, in conjunction with relevant organisations, of a common set of standards governing nurseries, registered childminders, nannies, day care, holiday and out-of-school schemes;

- the development of a mechanism for implementing and monitoring these standards nationally;
- funding;
- the coordination of the partnership of central government, employers, local authorities, and providers to ensure that each plays an active role appropriate to their abilities and resources;
- measurable criteria for the success of the strategy.

The 11 members of the Forum conclude:

> Childcare provision isn't only about enabling the individual to stay in the workplace. It is part of family, equality and labour market policies. As such, it involves different partners and requires the involvement of central Government to give it co-ordinated direction.

To date, there has been limited government response to this call despite there being little evidence to suggest that employers' resolve in this respect will weaken.

The European context

British policy and provision in relation to the conciliation of employment and family responsibilities is often unfavourably contrasted with that of other European countries (Hogg and Harker, 1992). Direct comparisons are difficult to make and indeed run the risk of oversimplification. However as Moss (1992) illustrates, the infrastructure of pre-school services in Britain differs markedly from that in most mainland European countries, some of the most significant differences being that in these:

- compulsory schooling generally begins at six years;
- prior to this, nursery education or kindergarten is publicly provided for most children from three upwards, and where this provision is not already virtually universal, there are active policies to expand;
- provision for children of three years and over is available for at least the equivalent of the British school day;
- provision for children under three years tends to be privately provided and funded;
- the public provision available for under threes tends to be group care (nurseries) although some countries also have systems of 'organised' childminding whereby local authorities or publicly

funded private organisations recruit, pay and support child-minders;
- every country in mainland Europe (with the exception of only Luxembourg) now offers some form of parental leave, lasting from a few weeks to two or more years.

In addition to these specific differences, Moss (1992), moreover, points out that the underlying approach to pre-school provision in Britain – of viewing the care and education of children as a mainly **private** matter – is fundamentally different to that of its European partners, the latter having

> been more influenced by concepts of social solidarity, emphasising the importance of providing support to adults in the parenting phase of their life course, which is recognised to be (like childhood) of wider social significance.

Significantly, however, in March 1992 Britain became a signatory to a *Recommendation* of the Council of the European Communities (92/241/EEC) which urged the taking of measures which would help parents reconcile the demands of work and family. Although the member states of the Community have no statutory obligation to implement the provisions of this Recommendation, they do have to inform the Commission within three years (that is, by March 1995) of the measures taken to give effect to the Recommendation, which focuses on four main areas: provision of child care services; special leave for employed parents; changes in the environment, structure and organisation of work, to make them more responsive to the needs of workers with children; the sharing of occupational, family and upbringing responsibilities between men and women.

So far as child care is concerned, the main points are:
- parents who are working, following a course of training, or seeking employment should have as much access as possible to local child care services;
- such services should be affordable to parents;
- services should combine care with general upbringing and a pedagogical approach;
- the needs of parents and children should be taken into account when access to services is determined;
- services should be available in all areas, both urban and rural;
- services should be available to children with special needs, for example, linguistic needs, and to children in single parent families;

- initiatives should encourage flexibility and diversity of child care services as part of a strategy to increase choice and meet the different preferences, needs and circumstances of children and their parents, whilst preserving coherence between different services;
- training of child care workers should be appropriate to the importance and social and educative value of their work;
- child care services should work closely with local communities;
- financial contributions to child care services should be encouraged from national, regional or local authorities, management and labour, other relevant organisations and private individuals.

Clearly, at the time of writing, the government's response is still awaited. Nonetheless, it is apparent that the above summary points have considerable implications for the development of pre-school services in Britain in terms of both accessibility and the form of service provided.

Whither nursery provision?

The aim of this chapter has been to place day care – and, more specifically, nurseries – within the context of early childhood services more generally. The imbalance between the demand for and public provision of day care has been noted, as has the more recent heightening of public interest in the matter and the consequent pressure for increased provision. Attention has also been drawn to the traditional distinction in this country between day care and pre-school education, with the former undergoing not only changes in the level of provision over the years but also changes of form.

This has certainly been the case with nursery provision. Even a brief perusal of the literature shows that at different points in time nurseries have offered full-time care, at other times sessional care; at some points they have been viewed as catering for the whole range of pre-school children (including babies), at other times for mainly three and four-year-olds, and at times they have been regarded as offering a service primarily for working mothers, at others as a form of compensatory parenting. Traditionally, too, nurseries had a health orientation: they were staffed by nursery 'nurses', under the overall supervision of a matron – a further contrast to nursery education which has always been teacher-led. These shifts in the form of nursery provision illustrate the remarkable ability of nurseries over the years to adapt to changing patterns of demand and thinking.

However, the cumulative effect of a number of more recent developments may mean that nurseries are now having to face their greatest challenge to date. Changes in the employment patterns of women have led to a demand for full-time places for babies unimaginable in the post-war Bowlby era of thinking. Also, at the older end of the age spectrum dealt with by nurseries, the introduction by the 1988 Education Reform Act of the National Curriculum has meant that nurseries and other forms of pre-school provision are under increasing pressure from some parents to follow a relatively narrow and rigid curriculum in preparation for school. Such a move would be quite at odds with the recommendations of the Rumbold Committee (Department of Education and Science, 1990) which examined the educational experience of children in a range of pre-school settings and concluded by rejecting the notion of a national subject-based curriculum for under fives. Nonetheless the Rumbold Committee did underline the importance of early years education and of curriculum planning in **all** settings, emphasising that 'the process of education – **how** children are encouraged to learn – is as important as, and inseparable from, the content – **what** they learn.' (DES, 1990).

Finally, the provisions of the 1989 Children Act are intended to represent a significant landmark in the history of pre-school services generally, including nursery provision. The Act leaves national policy in relation to levels of provision unchanged. However the new provisions in relation to registration, annual inspection and the triennial review of services are directed at improving the **quality** of provision. The Guidance accompanying the Act (Department of Health, 1991) therefore sets out six general principles which, it states, should underpin all day care, education and related services for young children and their families, these being:

- children's welfare and development are paramount;
- children should be treated and respected as individuals whose needs (including special educational needs) should be catered for;
- parents' responsibility for their children should be recognised and respected;
- the values deriving from different backgrounds – ethnic,

cultural, religious and linguistic – should be recognised and respected;

- parents are generally the first educators of their children; this should be reflected in their relationships with other carers and providers;
- parents should have easy access to information about services in their area and be able to make informed choices.

At a more practical level, the Guidance also sets **minimum** standards for each of the different types of early childhood services in relation to ratios, room size and space; record-keeping; health and safety and discipline. Local authorities, in turn, are expected to work with these minimum standards in establishing criteria to guide their registration and inspection functions within the local area.

As Pugh (1992) has pointed out the Guidance draws on the recommendations of the Rumbold Report and goes further than any previous government guidance in looking at curriculum issues, equal opportunities and matters relating to parental involvement. Whilst the introduction of guidance on each of these aspects has been wholeheartedly welcomed by experts in early childhood services, concern has been expressed about the chances of implementing this area of the Act. The curriculum, equal opportunities and parental involvement all challenge traditional modes of operating (if not thinking) and as such entail cultural change which will necessitate ongoing training and resources. Since the Act itself makes no provision for this, the question arises: 'How quickly will early childhood services – and nurseries in particular – be able to deal with these changes?'

2. Quality: what is it and can it be measured?

Definitions of quality and how it can be measured are clearly important considerations for research which evaluates services. For this reason, the research included an examination of the literature on this subject as it applies to nursery provision and to the early years field more generally. A growing concern with the issue of quality was revealed, and a consensus that it is a central factor in the development of services. Also highlighted was the multi-dimensional nature of quality and the considerable debate about the relative emphasis to be placed on measurable aspects of quality (see Williams, forthcoming). The purpose of this chapter, then, is to examine the development of thinking about quality in early years work and to describe how this has influenced our own approach to evaluating a particular group of nurseries.

Why the emphasis on quality?

The terms 'quality assurance', 'quality control', 'quality standards' and 'quality assessment' have become very familiar in the course of the past decade and are applied to products, services and procedures across the public, private and voluntary sectors. In the early years field, however, their emergence appears to be more than a simple, straightforward reflection of this general trend but to emanate from trying to take forward some of the more positive messages of research in pre-school services. For example, as we have noted, for many years much of such research – both in this country and elsewhere – has been concerned to assess the impact of day care attendance on children and to consider the relative advantages and disadvantages of different forms of provision. Thus, whilst research in the United States evaluating some specific pre-school programmes (see, for example, Lazar and others, 1982 and Berrueta and others, 1984) has shown quite clear relationships between attendance on programmes and improved performance in subsequent school careers, in Britain the messages from research have tended to be less clear. After reviewing a range of research evidence, Hennessey and others (1992), conclude that 'attending day care has no inherent effect on children, either for better or worse'. Likewise Sylva and David (1990) found that the different life pathways of individuals attending different forms of pre-school provision could not be attributed exclusively to that attendance.

Nonetheless, research – again carried out in Britain and elsewhere – has shown that children's development (cognitive, language, social and emotional) in day care is influenced by a range of diverse factors, which includes, for example, children's home circumstances, caregiver behaviour, and the stability of care experienced. In other words, the overall message of this body of research is that while **poor** care may be harmful, **good** care is beneficial. In terms of children's development, then, there has been a growing concern to ensure that the positive messages of research are carried through into practice and this has led to attempts to identify the constituents of 'quality' and to ensure that services are assessed according to developed criteria.

What has research contributed to our understanding of quality?

The aforementioned research stems largely from the North American tradition of developmental psychology and has made a distinctive contribution to our understanding of day care. For example, Clarke-Stewart (1991), summarising this contribution, identifies four different aspects of day care which appear to be significantly related to children's behaviour and development: the physical environment, the caregiver's behaviour, the curriculum and the number of children and adults in the group. As far as the physical environment is concerned (health and safety issues aside), research indicates that it is not so much the amount of physical space or the number of toys available but how the space is organised and having a variety of toys and materials which offer a range of educational experiences. Secondly, research has also shown that children's social and intellectual development can be influenced by the manner in which caregivers respond to children. For example, children's skills in this respect are promoted when their caregivers are:

- responsive (they answer the children's questions and respond to their requests);
- positive (giving praise, smiles, making life generally enjoyable);
- accepting (following the children's suggestions as well as listening to them, acknowledging effort, not just the child who gets it 'right');
- informative in their interactions with the children (giving reasons, explanations, lessons).

Some detailed research has also been carried out (notably Whitebook and others, 1989) on the conditions which are most likely to lead to responsive, positive, accepting and informative behaviour by caregivers, and here important links have been identified with staff training, salary and conditions of employment and the stability of the staff group.

A third area identified by research is the significance of adult/child ratios. Here research findings acknowledge the relevance of the age of the child but also point to the necessity of achieving a balance between the value children derive from having opportunities to interact with others of a similar age and their need for adult relationships and stimulation.

The fourth and final area highlighted by Clarke-Stewart concerns the curriculum. This aspect, encompasssing all the experiences and activities children have in the day care setting, is less straightforward. However, drawing on research from a range of different cultural settings, Sylva (1994) demonstrates that the context of young children's experience – how they are encouraged to learn – can have a long-term effect on the development of their cognitive and social skills, extending well beyond the pre-school years. In this respect, day care settings have much to learn from the field of early childhood education.

Clarke-Stewart also points out that on several of the foregoing dimensions, the relationship is a curvilinear one. In other words, past a certain point having, for example, more space, more toys, more stability or more training ceases to be advantageous. Relating this to the current US situation, she goes on to argue that efforts to improve services should therefore focus on defining minimum acceptable standards and ensuring that all day care meets these.

The quality debate

Those framing Part X of the Children Act dealing with day care in this country clearly shared much of the thinking of Clarke-Stewart and we now have minimum standards in relation to several of the measurable factors which day care research has shown as influencing children's development. The Act does, however, recognise the importance of other factors too in arriving at a definition of quality, and that these include the rights and expectations of children, parents and people working with young children. Melhuish (1991) outlining an approach to quality based on children's rights highlights how, depending on the values held by a society, the child may be regarded as having rights which go beyond the provision of an environment which can be empirically demonstrated to facilitate development. Likewise, a definition of quality which encompasses parents' rights would have to take account of parents' access to day care services, choice between services, transport to services and hours that child care is available. And similarly, given the crucial role that child care workers play in day care services, the case can be made for their rights to be taken into consideration in arriving at a definition of quality in relation to services.

The attention given to 'quality' and 'standard setting' by the Children Act, has led several organisations working in the pre-school field in this country to produce guidelines for good practice (see, for example, Kids' Clubs Network, 1991; National Child-minding Association, 1991; National Children's Bureau, 1991 and Pre-school Playgroups Association, 1993). Elfer and Wedge (1992) collectively describe these different recent initiatives aiming to define quality as 'quality frameworks'. They suggest there is a danger in the use of such frameworks in that they may focus attention on the framework itself, rather than the quality of the interaction with individual children. On the other hand, they argue, the key to the effectiveness of a quality framework is the extent to which it assists those working with children to evaluate their work continually. Whilst these authors acknowledge the importance of taking into account the findings of research, they also argue that a full under-standing of quality rests on recognising that:

- the concept of quality is meaningless unless it is related to the values and beliefs that underpin a service (or: it all depends what you think really matters!);
- in the provision of any service there may be a number of

'stakeholders' who could be considered as users, and other groups who may have a key interest in the way the service is provided (or: from whose point of view are we looking?);

- the review of quality needs to entail more than a review of the individual service and must include the policy and organisational framework within which a service operates (or: are we looking at the individual service or the whole system?);
- assessing quality must go beyond the application of checklists and frameworks (or: can you measure relationships?).

Attempting to arrive at a definition of quality acceptable across the diversity of services provided by the member states of the European Union, Balaguer and others (1991) also stress the importance of recognising underlying values and the need to take account of the perspectives of the different stakeholders or interest groups involved. Rejecting an approach which relies exclusively on measurable factors, these writers introduce their discussion paper commenting:

> Any definition of quality is to an extent transitory; understanding quality and arriving at quality indicators is a **dynamic** and **continuous** process of reconciling the emphases of different interest groups. It is **not** a prescriptive exercise. On the other hand it needs to be a detailed exercise which is of direct practical use to those working with young children. (p. 6)

In the first part of the paper ten key areas of quality are identified – accessibility, environment, learning activities, relationships, parents' views, the community, valuing diversity, assessment of children and outcome measures, cost benefits and ethos – and in relation to each of these a number of quality indicators is outlined. However, the writers then move on to discuss how quality can be assured and highlight the importance of recognising that setting standards at the local or 'micro' level is of limited value without standard setting at the 'macro' level also. In addition they point to the need for coordination across the micro and macro levels and to the key issues of policy, financing and resources, planning and monitoring, advice and support, staffing, training, physical resources, research and development, and the integration and coordination of services.

Both Balaguer and others and Elfer and Wedge emphasise, then, the importance of recognising the different values which underlie pre-school services and the need, in setting quality standards, to take account of the wider policy context in which individual services operate. Setting quality standards is, of course, no guarantee that these standards will be translated into practice by either practitioners or policy makers at the local or national level and for this reason, the value of the concept of 'quality' has been questioned by some researchers. Moss and Melhuish (1991), for example, suggest that the term 'quality' be retained only in relation to the way in which a service performs in achieving service objectives. One such service objective, they argue, would be the promotion of children's cognitive, language and social and emotional development but other objectives then need also to be defined for different groups of stakeholders such as parents and staff.

Our approach to this study

In designing this study, we have been mindful of the foregoing considerations and, insofar as the constraints of time imposed on any one research project allow, have attempted to give them due regard. Furthermore, from the various writings on values, we are clear that we need to make explicit the values which we bring to this research and in this respect, there appear to be three broad themes which we need to address. First and foremost, our main concern lies with children and, thus, whilst we also attempt to examine nurseries with the needs of parents and staff in mind, this is nonetheless from the perspective of how these ultimately impact on the service the child receives. Secondly, when thinking of services to young children which entail regular separation from parents for at least a minimum of several hours a day on a regular basis, we can see little sense in making a distinction between their care and their education: the two are inseparable and nurturing **all** aspects of a child's development is the core task. Finally, whilst we would certainly endorse the view that parents have duties and responsibilities as well as rights in relation to their children, we do not subscribe to the view that the care of children is a private matter: there should be public investment in assisting parents in their nurturing role and in ensuring that children have equal access to services which maximise their developmental potential.

These values appear to us to also underlie what Pugh has described as the main issues in providing good quality services for young children. These are listed in the training notes to a video (Barnardo's, 1992) as follows:

- the need for clearly defined aims and objectives;
- an effective management structure;
- a policy on equal opportunities, encompassing gender, ethnicity and disability, which promotes an understanding of cultural and physical diversity and challenges stereotypes;
- close relationships between staff and parents and the involvement of parents in the running of the nursery;
- an atmosphere in which every child and adult feels secure, valued and confident;
- good relationships between adults and children, between children and children, and between adults and adults;
- a broad, balanced and relevant curriculum, appropriate to the physical, social, emotional, spiritual and intellectual development of children, informed by observation and assessment of children;
- a system of record keeping which monitors children's learning and is shared with parents;
- evidence of children being actively involved in their learning, with a strong emphasis on play and talking;
- well trained staff who can understand and respond to the needs of individual children and structure and support their learning;
- a staff development plan which ensures access to regular support, supervision and training for all staff;
- a good ratio of staff to children, and small groups;
- a well organised physical environment, with access to appropriate resources both inside and outside, and due attention to health and safety;
- liaison with others involved in the child's health, care and education in the local community;
- a system for monitoring and review of provision.

Carrying out the research

As has already been mentioned in the Introduction, the study was designed to take place in two phases and a range of research methods was employed, including a postal survey in the first phase and interviews and observation in the second. This second phase provided us with the opportunity to look at 15 nurseries in some detail and to consider their 'performance' in relation to the foregoing criteria. However, some objective measure of performance was clearly necessary and for this purpose we made use of variations of an existing scale, the Early Childhood Environment Rating Scale (ECERS).

The ECERS was developed in the USA in the early 1980s by Harms and Clifford (1980) and designed to cover a range of early childhood group environments. Over the years it has been used in a number of other countries in a range of different settings (Statham and Brophy, 1992). One major adaptation of ECERS is that by McCail (1991) whose Pre-Five Environment Rating Scale was developed for use in Scottish pre-school educational settings but which has subsequently also been used by at least one other researcher in nurseries in England (Finch, 1993).

The term 'environment', as used in this and the original ECERS scale, is very broadly defined, such that it includes not only the use of space and materials but also the daily programme and the role of adults. The original ECERS comprised 37 individual items grouped into seven subscales; McCail introduced two further subscales; and we ourselves have added additional items such that the scale as we used it comprised 64 individual items grouped into nine subscales. At the stage of analysis some further amendments were made within some subscales but these are of no substantive concern in the current context (see Appendix 1 for details of the instrument as we used it).

The scale itself is based on each individual item being accorded a score of between 1 (inadequate) and 7 (excellent), definitions of what is appropriate at scores 1, 3, 5 and 7 being provided. In practice, items rarely fit the descriptions exactly, and so scores of 2, 4 or 6 can be awarded as appropriate. McCail emphasises that it is important to use the rating which **best fits** the situation, and that it must be applied to the current situation as found, not on plans for the future, or what it was like the week before.

In their original form, these scales were intended to be completed in a visit of only a few hours to an establishment, which we felt was inadequate to take serious account of the importance of interactions and relationships within a nursery setting. In addition to interviews with staff, we therefore undertook two distinct forms of observation. The first of these entailed undertaking general observations in each area of the nursery, at different times of the day and on different days. In addition to providing a general view of the nursery, this approach gave additional opportunities to note instances of anti-discriminatory practice in activities, behaviour and use of language; children making choices and planning for themselves and, finally, adult behaviour or language likely to enhance children's self-esteem or self-image.

The second form of observation undertaken was based on 'shadowing' specific children, selected to provide a range of ages in each nursery. In carrying out these observations, we adopted the Target Child approach, a technique first developed by Sylva and others (1980), and extended by others, including the Open University for their *Working with Under Fives* pack (1991). This approach involves 20-minute periods of constant observation of a child, recording in detail all interactions, noting the activity in which the child is involved, and with whom. By adopting this approach, we were able to examine in a systematic manner whether and how opportunities are created and taken to promote and encourage children's learning.

These two forms of observation – in combination with information from interviews and from examination of the records kept by nurseries – were used to complete the Environment Rating Scale we employed (referred to in subsequent chapters as ERS). In the chapters which follow, this data is considered alongside data from the 95 replies to the postal survey undertaken in the first phase of the research.

3. The nurseries: a brief pen picture

Given the very limited amount of information routinely collected on nurseries on a national basis, it is impossible to tell to what extent the group of nurseries we have dealt with is representative of nurseries as a whole. The purpose of this chapter, then, is to provide a brief outline description of the nurseries involved in the study: their similarities and differences in terms of, for example, ownership and management arrangements, whether they are registered with the local authority, the number of children they cater for and the fees they charge. The data is drawn from replies to the postal questionnaire which was sent to the 112 nurseries with which Midland Bank, at that time, had a 'partnership' arrangement: 95 nurseries responded to this questionnaire (an 85 per cent response rate) and this chapter is based on some of the information supplied by these nurseries.

In the sense that these 95 nurseries were offering some or all of their places to the children of working parents, they could be described as 'workplace nurseries'. However, that term tends to be reserved for nurseries which are directly provided by an employer or group of employers and which are often located in fairly close proximity to a parent's place of work. In this conventional use of the term, then, these are not a group of workplace nurseries, although, indeed, two of the total group of 95 were wholly-owned by the Bank (and managed separately on their behalf). What these nurseries do however have in common is their link with Midland Bank; and the Bank has drawn up a set of operational guidelines designed to demonstrate the standards of management and practice expected of all those with whom it has a partnership agreement, these being subject to continual review. Acknowledging this link and the fact that nurseries of the type generally provided by local authority social services departments (often known as 'family centres') may be under-represented in this sample, we have no reason to suspect that the group of nurseries we have dealt with form other than a broad cross-section of nurseries currently available across the public and private sectors.

Where were the nurseries located?

Table 3.1 shows the distribution of the 95 nurseries across England and Wales. The nurseries do not cluster around the London area – less than 20 per cent were London-based – but it must be remembered that these nurseries are included here because of their involvement with Midland Bank, whose own child care policy is based on business need. The geographical distribution of the nurseries, then, is a reflection of where the Bank has anticipated difficulty in recruiting and retaining staff.

Table 3.1 Regional distribution of nurseries

Region	No. of nurseries responding to questionnaire	No. of nurseries visited
North	28	4
South	21	1
Midlands	19	3
London	17	4
West	5	1
Wales	5	2
Total	95	15

The location of a nursery is an important consideration for working parents, who understandably prefer to minimise the journey time between home, nursery and workbase. They therefore have a preference for nurseries to be either close to home, or close to work, or en route between the two, rather than necessitating a major diversion or special journey. Information provided by the nurseries suggests that many parents have to compromise on this issue for the sake of having a nursery place. In practice, then, these nurseries did not tend to serve relatively well-defined geographical areas or communities but drew in 'customers' from a widespread area. Significantly, only 14 nurseries provided for an inner city population, where few people may actually live, although many travel daily to work there. Also, only four nurseries felt their clients came from a largely rural area, a reflection perhaps of the locality of Bank and other employer operations.

Table 3.1 also shows the distribution of the nurseries visited during the fieldwork phase of the research. Compared with the whole group, nurseries in Wales were somewhat over-represented, and in the South under-represented. Three nurseries were located in urban areas, four in suburban areas of large cities and eight in medium-sized towns.

Ownership and management of the nurseries

Whilst the nurseries responding to our questionnaire became involved in this study because of their link with Midland Bank, it is interesting to note that 82 of the 95 (over 85 per cent) had in any case originally been set up to meet the needs of a particular group of employees or, in the case of college and university nurseries, of students and staff. Of the 13 exceptions to this, two nurseries operated primarily as community nurseries, but also offered some places to particular groups of employees; two of those described in Table 3.2 as 'local authority' nurseries – whilst primarily accepting social services referrals – also reserved places for particular groups of employees; the private nurseries were generally open to all users (on the assumption that their fees could be met), but reserved some places for Midland Bank employees, and sometimes also for other companies' employees.

As Table 3.2 shows, the nurseries were provided by a range of different organisations and agencies, the largest single group being those set up by colleges or universities.

The way in which the nurseries were managed varied considerably, both within and between the above groups. Twenty-seven nurseries reported that a management committee or steering group, with parent representation, was responsible for overall management. Nine nurseries were managed by professional child care consultants such as Kinderquest, Kids Unlimited, Berkshire Childcare Consultancy, Little Urchins and Company Childcare. College and university nurseries were variously under the overall charge of the personnel department, the student services manager, the principal or vice-principal.

The contract which nurseries enter into with Midland Bank

Table 3.2   Nuseries by type of ownership

Type of ownership	Total number of nurseries	Number visited
College/university	44	6
Local authority	12	1
School	9	2
Private	9	1
Hospital/Health Authority	7	1
Chamber of Commerce/Partnership of employers	5	1
Single company	4	1
Government department	2	1
Community group	2	1
Employment project	1	0
Total	95	15

stipulates that there should be a nursery steering or management group, which includes representation from parents (not necessarily Midland parents) and also from a manager of a local Midland operation. In some circumstances this means that several 'levels' of management are in operation with a steering or management group, as recommended by the Bank, existing alongside, or in addition to, professional consultants, college staff or other managers. In this situation, one would have to question the extent to which a single parent representative would be in a position to influence effectively the overall management of the nursery. Furthermore, in the case of colleges where ultimate management responsibility lay with the college principal or vice-principal, there appeared to be a considerable risk of management being remote from the actual service.

Were the nurseries registered by the local authority?

Registration by local authority social services departments is the method employed by government of ensuring that certain minimum standards are achieved in day care. Whilst the majority of the nurseries described here were initially required to be registered under the provisions of the Nurseries and Childminders Regulation Act 1948, this legislation has now been superseded by Part X of the 1989 Children Act under whose provisions, nurseries were required to be re-registered by October 1992. Unfortunately, this meant that our questionnaire was being completed at the very time when local authorities were still involved in re-registering individual nurseries, with the result that only 52 of the 95 nurseries were able to say that they were currently registered.

Whilst registration and the complementary inspectorial function may understandably provoke some anxiety for nursery management and staff, it can also confer benefits in the sense that it may improve access to relevant support and training from the local authority. We were therefore surprised to find that at least two nurseries appeared to be considered as being exempt from registration under the new Act, despite the fact that they were located in colleges, and not in schools (the latter being specifically excluded from the registration requirement – Schedule 9, paras. 3 and 4, Children Act 1989). At the same time, two other nurseries – one in a local education authority school, the other in a National Health Service hospital, were registered, despite their right to exemption under the Act. It is unclear how such anomalies have arisen but their existence would seem to suggest the need for some further clarification of the requirements of the 1989 Children Act.

Of the 52 nurseries who had already been re-registered under the new legislation, 22 had had new requirements imposed on them. These requirements tended to have involved quite major increases in revenue expenditure on, for example, additional staffing – or to have resulted in a diminished income since the number of places the nursery was registered to provide had been reduced. Some nurseries had also been required to make a substantial capital outlay to provide, for instance, a baby changing room or area or additional toilets and washbasins.

How long had the nurseries been operating?

On the whole, this was a very new group of nurseries with only seven having been open for more than three years and with two thirds having opened in the past two years. Not surprisingly, then, we received few reports of significant changes having been made to the way individual nurseries were run or the services they provided. Those changes a few nurseries did refer to included the introduction of holiday and after-school care, meeting the requirements of the Children Act (for example, in terms of increased staffing), extending premises in order to increase the number of places available and improving outdoor play space.

How many children did the nurseries provide for?

Overall, these 95 nurseries provided a total of 3,215 full-time equivalent (FTE) places. However as Fig 3.1 shows, the size of the nurseries, in terms of the number of places they offered, varied considerably: one offered only ten places, whilst several others provided in excess of 50. Overall, approximately half the nurseries provided 30 or fewer places, whilst more than 25 per cent provided in excess of 40 places (FTE).

Although the number of places provided varied considerably (see Fig 3.2), each of the 95 nurseries provided some places for under-twos, this being a requirement of Midland Bank in order to ensure continuity of employment following maternity leave. Almost one third of the total 3,215 places provided by the nurseries were for children under two.

With women returning to work soon after the birth of their baby, there is now a considerable and increasing demand not only for places for under-twos, but also for babies under a year old. Several nurseries remarked on this trend in completing the questionnaire, some also adding that their local social services department had placed restrictions on the number of baby places they could make available. However, we ourselves were unable to obtain accurate figures on the number of baby places being provided as nurseries tended to provide detailed information in terms of children aged under- or over-two years only.

The foregoing figures relate, of course, to the number of full-time equivalent places provided by the nurseries. However, not all children attend nursery on a full-time basis: some, for example, attend daily but for only a few hours on each occasion, others attend for a full day but not every day of the week. Indeed, one third of the nurseries intimated that the children they dealt with attended mainly on a part-time basis. In practical terms, then, this meant that the number of children attending some nurseries in the course of a week was frequently considerably greater than that implied by the figure for the number of places provided. This was particularly the case with college-based nurseries one of which, for example, was registered for six children under-two and 20 over-two, but which

Figure 3.1   Number of FTE places in nurseries

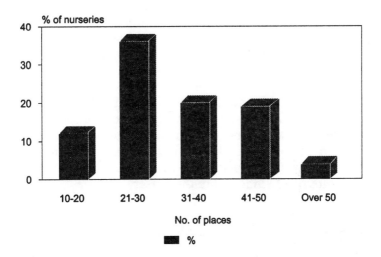

Figure 3.2   Number of places for under-twos in nurseries

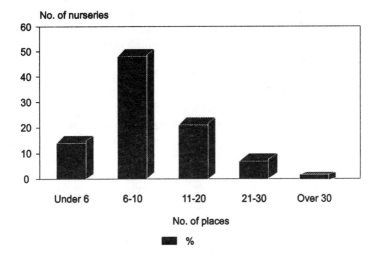

actually had 12 under-twos and 49 over-twos on the register, a total of 61 different children passing through the nursery in the course of a week. Whilst nurseries obviously have to maintain a certain level of 'occupancy' to be economically viable and must also be able to offer a flexible response to the needs of individual families, the mix of full and part-time children raises important issues about how nurseries structure their services for individual children. We return to this theme subsequently but for the moment draw attention to what seems to be a practical dilemma for many nurseries: the role of the nursery in the life of a child who attends for up to 50 hours per week will be significantly different to that for a child who attends for perhaps less than six hours – what implications does this have for the curriculum offered to each, for key worker roles and for the underlying importance placed on the stability and continuity of relationships of all kinds within the nursery setting?

The hours nurseries are available

For those parents who work, the hours a nursery is open is an important factor which has to take account of parents' own hours of work (which may entail shift work) as well as the time involved in the return journey between home and nursery and nursery and the workplace. Both the actual distance involved and traffic congestion can mean that such journeys are very time-consuming and it is in acknowledgement of this that Midland Bank suggests to the nurseries with whom it has a partnership arrangement that they should be open between the hours of 8.00 a.m. and 6.30 p.m. for a minimum of 50 weeks of the year.

The postal questionnaire information suggests that the vast majority of nurseries (88) were available for 50 weeks of the year and of the remaining seven, four were open for 49 weeks and three for 48 weeks. Generally speaking, too, the weeks of closure were arranged to coincide with the Christmas and Easter public holiday periods, thus minimising disruption to parents' work commitments.

A rather less uniform picture emerges in relation to the daily hours of opening. Here the core hours appeared to be between 8.00 a.m. and 6.00 p.m. – a total of ten hours – and over 80 per cent of the nurseries described themselves as providing a service covering these times. In addition, 14 of these nurseries also reported opening earlier than 8.00 a.m. and six that they closed later than 6.00 p.m. That nurseries are open for such extended periods is undoubtedly a reflection of their effort to provide a flexible service aimed at meeting parents' needs for day care. However our observations in nurseries showed that, although it was not necessarily common, it was not unusual for individual children, including babies, to attend the nursery throughout the nursery day meaning that they could be attending for ten or more hours a day, five days a week. We are unaware of any research which has looked at the impact on children of home and nursery in these circumstances, but, like a number of the nursery staff we interviewed, we believe that such a situation gives rise to some fundamental questions concerning children's welfare, the respective roles of parents and nurseries in relation to children's upbringing and the obligations of employers to take account of family life and responsibilities.

Were all the nursery places used?

Although our postal survey attempted to explore the demand for places experienced by individual nurseries, the timing of the questionnaire – in the summer months – was somewhat unfortunate in that it was not only the holiday period but the time of year when most nurseries experience some downturn in numbers with children leaving the nursery to go to school and the September intake not yet being finalised. Furthermore, in the case of college nurseries, the academic year had ended and the demand for places from both staff and students had consequently diminished. Notwithstanding this, almost 35 per cent reported having no vacancies. Of the remainder, 21 stated that having vacancies was not typical, and referred variously to the effects of the recession, a recent increase in the number of places they provided, and the decision to keep numbers low pending staff recruitment.

More generally, however, it was clear that some nurseries always tended to have a few vacancies, whilst for others it was rare to run with more than a few spare sessions per week. Furthermore, although nine nurseries reported that current vacancies were in employer-reserved places, overall the trend was for unfilled places to occur in the over-two age range. This again underlines the current demand on nurseries to provide places for babies and toddlers.

Nursery fees

Wide variation was found amongst the 95 nurseries in relation to the fee-charging structure they operated. Some nurseries, for example, operated sliding scales whilst others charged on the basis of whether a child was under or over-two, and in college nurseries, different rates applied to staff and students. Furthermore, nurseries applied different charging bases – per week, per day, per hour, per session, and so forth. For the purpose of comparison, then, in Figure 3.3 below the fees listed are calculated on the basis of a maximum per week for a full-time place (5 x eight-hour days, or 10 sessions per week, or a 40-hour week).

Figure 3.3   Fees per full-time week

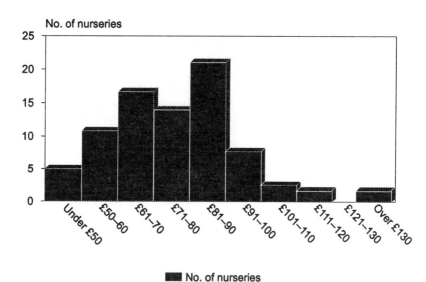

Clearly, then, a wide range of fees is charged by these nurseries – from under £50 to over £130 per week and with three quarters of the 95 nurseries charging up to £90 a week. Without employer support, such fee charges would be beyond the means of many parents.

Discussion

The purpose of this chapter has been to provide a broad picture of the group of nurseries involved in the research. It will have become evident that they represent a rather heterogenous group in many respects. However, notwithstanding their differences in terms of ownership, size and fees charged, many of the day-to-day issues raised in managing the nurseries are similar: providing a suitable curriculum for a range of children of different ages, who may spend differing amounts of time at the nursery; maintaining a flexibility to parental needs and simultaneously ensuring that the nursery is run efficiently, with places occupied but in line with the standards imposed by the local authority registration process. As has already been intimated in this chapter, the task of balancing these aspects is one which at times may involve a conflict between the needs and interests of parents and those of children.

4. Running a nursery: management, staffing and policy issues

People who work in nurseries tend to do so because they enjoy being with young children. However, there can be few adults who would deny that looking after young children – especially in numbers – is a very exhausting and demanding activity. Working in a nursery setting also means that you have to work with other adults – colleagues as well as parents – so communication and a shared understanding of how decisions are taken become important factors in ensuring the smooth running of the organisation. Furthermore, as we have already pointed out, recent years have seen increased expectations of nurseries in terms of, for example, fulfilling a role which goes beyond the physical care of children and taking account of the values which derive from different backgrounds in a diverse society – ethnic, cultural, religious and linguistic. This chapter, then, seeks to examine the organisational arrangements the sample nurseries currently had in place in order to cope with this situation in terms of policy, management and staffing. In this regard, having a clear view of the purpose of an organisation – and regularly reviewing how it performs in relation to this – are generally regarded as essential prerequisites. The chapter therefore begins with a consideration of this aspect of nursery organisation.

The aims and objectives of the nurseries

The postal questionnaire asked individual nurseries to describe the aims of the nursery in a few sentences and to include any documentation they had produced in this respect. The majority of nurseries (88) reported having a leaflet or booklet describing the nursery, and that this was available to parents. These leaflets varied tremendously in style and content to the extent that it is difficult to make generalised comments about them: the descriptions given on the questionnaire appear, therefore, to provide a better basis on which to obtain an overall view. The following examples give a flavour of how nurseries described their aims:

> To provide a safe, happy, secure environment for all children. To encourage individual development. To help and encourage children to develop self-esteem and confidence and to become effective communicators.

> To provide a high and consistent standard of childcare to meet parents' and children's needs.

> To offer high quality childcare which upholds the basic principles of good practice for children, parents and staff, with the objective of giving each child every opportunity to grow and develop.

> Highest standard of care. Happy, caring, safe environment in which children can achieve their own potential. Stimulating types of play. Trusting relationship with parents, make the nursery welcoming.

Not surprisingly, some phrases tended to recur across the range of nursery replies. For example, between 30 and 40 nurseries referred in their aim to providing 'quality care'; to a 'happy' or 'stimulating' environment, and to 'work with parents'. Rather less reference was made to the need for a 'safe' environment and to meeting the individual needs of each child, while some 15 to 20 nurseries described their objective in terms of providing a 'warm', 'loving' or 'secure' environment for children. Very few respondents, however, made any reference to preparing children for school, to the educative value of the nursery provision or to encouragement of children's confidence, self-esteem and independence. Describing the atmosphere desirable in the nursery, the expressions 'ordered', 'calm', 'relaxed' and 'family atmosphere' were quite frequently employed. Others nurseries, however, appeared to wish to convey a more dynamic atmosphere, saying the nursery should be 'interesting', 'fun', 'creative' and 'present challenges'. Moreover, considering the emphasis placed by the 1989 Children Act on the need to respect culture and ethnicity, there were surprisingly few references to issues to do with equal opportunity or cultural difference and diversity. Likewise, only four nurseries referred to their intention to provide for the needs of staff, in terms of enabling them to reach their full potential, having access to training and personal development programmes, and so forth.

There are clearly limitations to drawing conclusions from such generalised statements: aims and objectives are inevitably somewhat general when concisely expressed and their 'meaningfulness' is very dependent on the extent to which they are translated into practice. Although significant omissions do suggest priorities, a striking feature of the responses is the wide diversity and range of qualities referred to and it is interesting to consider whether the same request to nursery schools would elicit a similarly varied list of statements.

Nurseries were also asked to describe any more detailed or specific plans or targets they had for the forthcoming year and these replies give, perhaps, a clearer picture of the priorities being identified. Some of the newer nurseries, for example, were concerned to maximise the use of their existing facilities and referred to filling their complement of places. Several of these, as well as some from the wider group, also described plans to expand the scope of their services by, for example, developing a holiday playscheme and/or after-school care, or expanding and improving their outdoor play space. Within this context, too, staff development programmes, making more links with the local community, developing the curriculum, making better links with parents and improving children's developmental records were also identified as areas requiring change but these were mentioned by relatively few nurseries. Likewise a small number specifically mentioned the need to meet the requirements of the Children Act, or to improve their procedures in order to achieve the requirements of the quality assurance standard BS5750.

The questionnaire also invited respondents to indicate whether they experienced any particular difficulties in achieving the overall aims of the nursery. In this context, only a few nurseries (11) made reference to resources per se but a range of other difficulties was mentioned which highlight the complexity of the task of managing a nursery. For example, many nurseries drew attention to the constraints imposed on them by the limitations of space which meant, amongst other things, that they were unable to group children within the nursery in the manner which they thought was most appropriate. A further group of difficulties identified included issues in relation to time management and administrative systems. The former was raised by a range of nurseries and the point being made – mainly by nursery managers – appeared to be 'how does one fit it all in?' Administrative difficulties seemed to be most acutely felt by nurseries managed at 'arms length' by a head office or County

Hall, and by college and health authority nurseries. Such nurseries commented on the cumbersome and inefficient nature of management and administrative procedures which variously led to delays in staff payments, in decision-making generally and to planning staff rotas. However, the most frequently mentioned group of difficulties related to staffing: for example having sufficient flexibility within the staffing quota to be able to cover particularly busy times of the day, holiday periods and sick leave; having adequate time to be able to hold staff meetings; ensuring that the nursery manager had adequate 'office' time; staff conditions of employment generally, and having a more generous adult:child ratio for the very youngest children. Interestingly, too, several nurseries referred in this context to the difficulty of generating and maintaining staff morale, given the low status accorded to nursery staff. In particular, two school-based nurseries referred to the perceived contrast in status between staff working in the nursery and teaching staff in the school.

Evaluating aims and objectives

Nurseries' recognition of the importance of regularly reviewing their achievement of aims and objectives was evident from responses to the postal questionnaire whereby the vast majority of respondents (86) claimed to have some form of evaluation procedure in place. For the most part, however, these were relatively informal procedures based on existing practices such as staff meetings, advisory group meetings and management committee meetings. Indeed only 12 nurseries described what appeared to be specifically designed self-evaluation procedures which incorporated, for example, annual questionnaires to staff, annual appraisal of nursery services, an annual management conference, or an operations policy or service plan reviewed and revised on an annual basis and a linked quality assurance process. Whilst in this context a few nurseries made reference to the existence of a complaints/compliments book whereby parents could communicate their views to the nursery management, none actually mentioned formal consultation of parents as an integral part of the evaluation process.

Our site visits confirmed that most nurseries tend to approach evaluation in this rather unstructured and informal manner. For example, rating the nurseries in this respect on the Environment Rating Scale (ERS), only one nursery achieved the 'Excellent' score since annual evaluation was undertaken by the whole group, including management, staff and parents; broad aims and the means by which they were to be achieved were set out, and the evaluation, in written form, was available to all concerned with the nursery. A further five nurseries did receive the 'Good' rating since, as well as there being some form of annual evaluation by the management group involving the setting of objectives, there was also regular room evaluation linked to forward planning. Of the nine remaining nurseries, two of which received an 'Inadequate' rating, there was either no evaluation at all or it was sporadic and staff-initiated, perhaps involving parents but only to a limited degree.

It would appear from this, then, that only a few of the nurseries operated within a framework of clear aims and objectives and a means whereby these could be reviewed and revised. For the remainder of the nurseries, the absence of such a framework has implications not only in terms of their ability to achieve generally agreed minimum standards, but also in the sense that there is an increased dependence within the nursery itself on communication and shared understanding between the staff group. Before looking at this in further detail, we turn first to consider staffing and then the more detailed policies devised by the nurseries.

Over the years, the personal and professional attributes of those providing non-parental care of children has drawn public attention and in recent times, this attention has focused on those who provide residential care for children and young people (for example Department of Health, 1992). However, writers in the pre-school field (for example, Whitebook and others, 1989; Moss and Melhuish, 1991, and Pugh, 1992) have consistently drawn attention to the relatively low status of nursery school teachers and day care workers. Indeed, in addition to highlighting the influence of staff turnover on children's social and language development, Whitebook's research revealed that of all the adult work environment variables examined, staff wages were the single most important predictor of quality. The Guidance to the Children Act (Department of Health, 1991) takes on board the implications of such research to the extent that recommendations are made about staff training and qualifications and attention is drawn to the rights of people working with young children. How, then, do the nurseries appear to be faring in this respect?

Staff numbers and recruitment

The number of staff a nursery employs is determined, of course, by the number of children it deals with and the registration require-ments, in terms of adult:child ratios, of the local authority in which it is based. These ratios are discussed in some detail in chapter 6. In the current context, we would nonetheless draw attention to two significant aspects of staffing revealed by the postal survey of nurseries: the very low proportion of male staff and the relatively extensive use of part-time staff. For example, out of a total staff group of 982, only eleven were male – one per cent overall. Furthermore, whilst over the nursery group as a whole 27 per cent of the staff were employed on a part-time basis, this figure masks quite considerable individual differences. For example, in 11 nurseries more than half the staff group were part time. Given the emphasis placed in child development literature (see chapter 2) on continuity of care and carer and on having appropriate role models available, these characteristics have implications for the type of relationships the nurseries concerned are able to offer to children. Moreover, the apparent reliance placed on part-time staff by some nurseries has more general implications for communication within the nursery.

By means of the questionnaire to all nurseries, we attempted to identify the qualities sought when recruiting staff. Because we intentionally left respondents to describe these qualities in their own words, a lengthy list of attributes was engendered. However, the following characteristics give some flavour of the responses, each of these having been mentioned by at least ten respondents, and being presented here in order of decreasing frequency:

- caring;
- enthusiasm/keen/lively/energetic/bright;
- commitment to team work;
- flexibility/adaptability;
- warmth/friendliness/cheerfulness;
- conscientious/dedicated/committed/motivated;
- sense of humour;
- can use initiative/creative/imaginative;
- patience;
- sensitivity/awareness of individual needs;
- reliability/honesty/integrity;
- enjoyment or love of children;
- good communication skills;

- understanding of equal opportunities issues.

Although they were mentioned rather less frequently, the following attributes were also referred to fairly consistently: 'a responsible attitude', 'kindness', 'confidence', 'cleanliness', 'smart appearance', 'maturity', 'non-judgemental attitude', 'common sense', 'organised' and 'flair'. As can be seen, there is at least one very significant omission from the list: the need to have an understanding of, and the ability to be responsive to, the needs of parents. Only two nurseries made reference to this increasingly important aspect of the job.

Furthermore, whilst an understanding of equal opportunities issues was described by several nurseries as a desirable attribute of staff, two thirds of the group overall reported having an all white staff group. Likewise, although not all nurseries gave information on the ethnic and cultural background of the children attending their facility, the data which is available shows that at least one third were dealing with children from black and minority ethnic groups, and in some instances (eight), such children represented more than 20 per cent of the total group. Having said this, 25 nurseries did report that at least one member of staff was able to converse in one of a range of Asian languages and equally, not all nurseries were located in ethnically diverse areas and might thus experience difficulty in recruiting minority ethnic staff. Nonetheless, it seems likely that nurseries generally may need to give more priority to this aspect of staff recruitment.

Nurseries were also asked whether they encountered any difficulty in recruiting staff. Somewhat surprisingly, less than 20 per cent (16) said that they did and in so saying, drew attention to low wages, long and unsociable hours, and shift work as the reasons for this. Only two respondents commented that it was sometimes difficult to find suitably qualified staff, and five that they were not always able to appoint staff who matched the high standards they sought. Several nurseries did, however, take the opportunity presented by this question to draw attention to the delay frequently created whilst awaiting police checks to be undertaken on potential employees.

Staff qualifications and training

The Children Act Guidance recommends that officers-in-charge and their deputies should hold a relevant qualification in child care, early years education, social work, health visiting or children's nursing and that at least half the staff should be qualified in child care, early years education or social work. In addition, it is recommended that all unqualified child care staff should be encouraged to undertake relevant training courses. As Table 4.1 shows, this particular group of nurseries had a relatively high proportion of trained staff. Not only did more than a third (37) have a staff group in which **all** staff had an appropriate qualification but even in those (57) where some staff were unqualified, this did not ever exceed half the total. In addition, the staff group of more than 25 per cent of the nurseries (25) included at least one member of staff with a teaching qualification, although not necessarily the early years specialism.

Table 4.1   Staff qualifications

	No. of nurseries	%
Mix of qualified and unqualified	57	60
All qualified	37	39
No data	1	1
Totals	95	100

A very high proportion (95 per cent) of nurseries responding to the postal questionnaire reported staff undertaking training during the previous year. In one instance, staff worked through an in-house training manual designed by a professional child care management company but otherwise training tended to comprise attendance on short courses or seminars on, for example, First Aid, the Children Act, AIDS/HIV, basic food hygiene, child abuse, gender and sexism, 'race awareness', listening skills, counselling, equal opportunities, special needs and conductive education.

However, given that there is now a requirement for staff to be regularly trained in First Aid and food and hygiene, it is perhaps not surprising that these featured so strongly in the list of training undertaken. Furthermore, although almost all nurseries had sent some staff on training, on closer examination, it is quite apparent that many staff had not had access to any training during the year and that there were limited opportunities for involvement in longer-term courses: for example, over the group as a whole, only four individuals were undertaking the NNEB Diploma in Post-Qualifying Studies or the diploma course of the Pre-school Playgroups Association. Some nurseries also drew attention to training completed by senior staff: here reference was made to courses on management, recruitment, team building, and customer care in relation to procedures leading to BS5750.

Although we did not collect information on staff experience of child care work in the postal questionnaire, we did attempt to include this alongside training and qualifications in the course of site visits. In this respect it was interesting to note that three of the 15 nurseries employed only staff with a child care qualification (including NNEB, NAMCW, BTec and PPA), and five included at least one person with a teaching qualification amongst the staff group. Indeed, in one nursery the part-time teacher, as well as working with different groups of children herself, had a very specific and influential role in helping staff plan and develop the curriculum. Site visits also allowed us to explore the extent to which opportunities were created for all staff to benefit from the experience of individual staff members who had attended short courses by, for example, feeding information into team meetings. Practice, in this respect, was very mixed and there seemed to be a strong reliance on informal communication.

Rating the 15 nurseries on the ERS resulted in ten fulfilling the 'Good' or above criteria, 'Good' being defined as staff, between them, having qualifications and experience covering children's development and play; practical aspects of children's play; working wih adults, including parents; children's health, safety and nutrition; and aspects of child protection. In addition, the manager in each of these nurseries appeared to have a good working knowledge of all of these areas and a specialised knowledge in at least one. Seven of those ten nurseries were accorded a better than 'Good' rating on the basis that, in addition to the foregoing, there was evidence of staff taking advantage of training to extend and update their knowledge and skills. As for the remaining five nurseries, the researchers tended to feel that they were 'not quite good enough' to be accorded a 'Good' rating. In most instances, this was because although some staff members did display the appropriate attributes in terms of qualifications, experience and training, a significant number did not and their behaviour and actions demonstrated a less than adequate understanding of children and their needs. Examples of this would include staff who consistently issued orders to children, who consistently missed opportunities to engage individual children in conversation and who tended generally to relate to children only as a group, rather than as individuals. Moreover, in these nurseries some staff did complain that it tended to be the nursery manager or deputy who always attended courses and that they – the staff group – received very little feedback.

Staff development: support, supervision and appraisal

While attendance at training courses is one way of promoting staff development, there are also other forms ranging from reading and membership of professional associations to more formal systems of supervision and appraisal provided by the employing agency. In the postal questionnaire, then, we enquired about the extent to which staff had access to periodicals or journals and almost 80 per cent of the nurseries responded by listing a range of magazines and journals which would assist staff in keeping abreast of developments in their field. It would have to be said that on site visits, we did not always see much evidence of such literature but this may be accounted for by the limitations of space (see later) and, as some college-based nurseries pointed out, such resources were available through an off-site library. Clearly, too, some staff take a more personal responsibility for this type of development and, in this respect, we were interested to note that 17 nurseries reported having some staff with individual membership of the specialist Professional Association of Nursery Nurses (PANN) or the National Association of Nursery Nurses (NANN). Furthermore six nurseries reported being affiliated to the National Association of Nurseries in Colleges, Universities and Polytechnics (NANCUP).

Also through the postal questionnaire, we endeavoured to explore the extent to which staff supervision and staff appraisal was part of standard nursery practice. In so far as the former was concerned, half (48) the nurseries indicated that supervision was built into the nursery programme, 17 stating that it was provided weekly, one every two weeks, 18 on a monthly basis and 12 every six weeks.

In the remaining 47 nurseries, the situation was not always entirely clear. In a few of these, the nursery manager appeared to be unconvinced of the need for supervision or had an inadequate grasp of the purpose of supervision and would typically respond to our question in the following manner:

> All staff well qualified, and can work without individual supervision.

> New procedures are taught as they arise, and this is ongoing.

> All qualified, so I keep this to a minimum.

More commonly, however, it appeared that while nursery managers recognised the importance of supervision, they found it very difficult to provide it on a regular basis, commenting for example:

> Time is the enemy and the unexpected happens.

> Due to demands on time and the shift system, this is difficult to schedule.

With regard to staff appraisal, only six of the 95 nurseries reported not having a system in place, the following comment being made by one of these:

> Don't believe in it – if there are problems they are dealt with!

However even amongst the 89 nurseries claiming to have an appraisal system, there seem to be grounds for querying the extent to which this was a formal and regular procedure. For example, nurseries located in colleges, schools, hospitals or business companies had quite frequently adopted the appraisal procedure of their 'host' organisation, and thus could be said to have a formal procedure. However, it was clear that for many nurseries, appraisal constituted little more than 'a chat' or a supervision session in which training needs and/or staff development more broadly might be discussed.

The foregoing negative picture of nurseries' approach to staff development is usefully examined in the context of our observations on, and questionnaire responses to, the subject of management style within the nursery. Both these exercises revealed an emphasis on attempting to adopt a 'team approach' which was quite striking. There was of course some degree of variation in this and not all staff subscribed to the view that they were equally involved in decision-making, but overall the style of management practised within the nurseries could certainly not be described as hierarchical. Commenting on the role of the nursery organiser, Goldschmeid and Jackson (1994) point out that the style of leadership favoured in many countries is a collegiate model, whereby a group of equal professionals share leadership in rotation. Of Britain, however, they say:

> ...we are only just emancipating ourselves from the strictly hierarchical structure inherited from the time when day nurseries were run like miniature hospitals.

What we appear to have observed are some of the tensions and 'teething troubles' encountered in this process of transition. For example, despite what we have described in terms of the absence of formal systems of support and appraisal, the impression we gained from site visits was, on the whole, of very enthusiastic and highly motivated staff groups, whose individual members did feel that they were involved in the running of the nursery. Furthermore, this sense of involvement appeared to derive as much from the very 'hands on' approach of most nursery managers, as it did from more formal attempts to promote staff participation. Thus, although only a few nurseries were able to organise meetings of the whole staff group – and then only very infrequently – the staff generally managed to share thoughts and arrive at understandings by a range of rather less formal methods, at the beginning and end of the day, during breaks and via relatively informal room meetings.

This 'on the hoof' form of planning, decision-making and communication did, however, have drawbacks. For example, not only did it mean that staff were quite often deprived of individual support, supervision and appraisal but it had implications for planning in many aspects of nursery functioning. A preoccupation with day-to-day activities or events in the fairly immediate future often resulted, with few opportunities for considered reflection of the daily programme for children; monitoring and recording children's progress; developing specific programmes for individual children and longer-term staff training needs. Very few nurseries, for instance, had adopted what is now accepted practice for schools: that of regularly closing the facility down and having a 'staff' day. Whilst the nursery manager's role in this respect is critical, it is doubtful whether taking this organising/coordinating role is possible when nursery managers assume such a major role in day-to-day activities. Indeed it is in recognition of this that Department of Health Guidance (1991) in relation to adult:child ratios states that the nursery manager's post should be counted as supernumerary in nurseries offering 20 or more places. It may be that nursery management committees have to do more to facilitate moves in this direction.

Staff working conditions

General conditions

Data from the postal questionnaire demonstrate the low salaries and relatively poor conditions of service experienced by many child care workers. For example, although some wide differences were noted, qualified nursery nurses in non-managerial posts were unlikely to be receiving more than £10,500 per annum (and frequently much less) and some nursery assistants were paid as little as £5,500 per annum. The majority of nurseries used local government scales but a few used nursing scales (Whitley Council). Of the remainder, two nurseries reported using LEA scales (but it was not clear whether this was for all staff, or only those with a teaching qualification), eight nurseries had their own scales, two had no scales and one private nursery volunteered that they paid at the rate of only £2.94 per hour. So far as annual leave was concerned, the majority (84) reported a minimum allocation of 20 days leave per year, and often more, with annual leave entitlement increasing with length of service. The private nursery referred to above stated that staff had just 12 days annual leave.

The staff of 83 nurseries had written job descriptions and in a further 11, some, but not all, staff were so provided (one nursery gave no information). Furthermore, although four nurseries stated that they did not provide part-time and casual staff with written contracts of employment, these appeared to be exceptions. In most nurseries, staff were reported to have access to their own personal files.

Hours of work and non-contact time

With only two exceptions, the nurseries operated a shift system. This varied from a relatively simple 'early, standard, late' system worked in rotation by staff, to enormously complex systems with a wide variety of starting and finishing times. Shift systems, in combination with the relatively high numbers of part-time staff, meant that there were likely to be frequent changes of staff in the course of the day, as well as day-to-day. Notwithstanding the impact of these changes on children's experience, managing this staff rota appropriately represents a considerable – and time consuming – challenge.

The energy, stamina, and patience required in working daily with very young children is such that it seems likely that one's capacity to perform the task optimally will reduce in the course of the day. Although the Children Act Guidance offers no suggestions in this respect, one set of good practice guidelines (National Children's Bureau, 1991) suggests that six hours a day should be the maximum, which then allows time for any necessary administrative tasks, as well as equally important planning and review activities. In the survey, 85 per cent of nurseries responded that some or all of their staff worked seven or seven and a half hours per day in direct child contact, with a further eight per cent quoting eight or more hours for some staff. In contrast, only slightly more than half the group reported allowing staff some official non-contact time, and this rarely amounted to more than a maximum of one or two hours per week, and was often used for meetings rather than planning or recording tasks.

The low priority accorded non-contact time was also evident when visiting the smaller group of 15 nurseries. In only five of these did staff have at least one hour per week designated for planning and recording and in a further two, not only was no time allocated, but there was no expectation on staff to plan activities ahead or to write up records. In the remaining eight nurseries, just over half, staff had no designated non-contact time and undertook planning and recording 'as and when they could' – during quiet times at the nursery or at home. In a couple of these nurseries it was reported that it was hoped to introduce better arrangements in the near future. Undoubtedly this situation must mean that there is a general absence of planning in nurseries, a feature which is highly unlikely to be in children's interests but which only nursery management has the authority to address.

Adult personal space
Whilst undoubtedly the primary function of the nursery premises is to service the needs of the children attending it, this function cannot be entirely separated from taking account of the needs of staff working there: for example, staff need to have occasional breaks away from the children; they need office space both to undertake paperwork and to store reference material; they need facilities for uninterrupted and private discussion both between staff and with parents; and they need a place where they can store their personal

belongings. The postal questionnaire revealed that many nurseries are very poorly equipped in this respect and that conditions within the nursery were the source of a great deal of staff dissatisfaction. In many nurseries, for example, there was only one room reserved as a non-child area, this having to function as office, staff room, interview room and parents' room. More specifically, a third of nurseries reported having no staff room facility: breaks therefore had to be taken in the office (with the potential then for being interrupted or disrupting someone else), in the kitchen (if this was large enough and had seating accommodation), outside (weather permitting) or, in the case of some school and college-based nurseries, offsite in a staff room or canteen. Likewise, less than half the group provided lockable storage space for staff belongings: purses, wallets and so forth as well as outdoor clothing. In three nurseries there was no office at all and a further 25 per cent described their current facility as quite inadequate, primarily in terms of its size.

This low level of provision for staff was also evident when visiting nurseries, with only three of the 15 achieving a 'Good' or higher rating on the ERS. In one nursery, for example, the manager's office doubled as a baby sleeping area, and the staff room doubled as a laundry room. In another, rather than going off-site, staff used the children's child-sized toilets. Overall, then, 12 nurseries were assessed as being in the range 'Inadequate' to not quite 'Good', the six who fell into this latter category being nurseries where one or more adult-only areas were available, but these were restricted by their size to a limited range of uses, and were, in any case, already multi-functional. The one nursery rated as 'Inadequate' had no special adult areas, no storage for adults' personal belongings, and no suitable area during the day for either individual consultations or for adult group meetings. Whilst in one respect it is highly commendable that nurseries give (as they appear to) such high priority to children's needs in allocating space, it nonetheless seems unfortunate that staff are rarely provided with appropriate – and customary – staff facilities. Indeed, it seems likely that the current arrangements have an adverse effect on the ability of staff to carry out their task optimally: the impact of the lack of facilities on planning and maintaining records, for example, would appear to be particularly significant.

Stability of the staff group

In order to assess the stability of the staff group, and hence the continuity of care and carers for children, nurseries were asked about the length of staff service, the number of staff who had left during the last two years and the current number of staff vacancies. Given that two thirds of this group of nurseries had been operational for less than two years, it is perhaps not surprising that more than 70 per cent (68) of nursery managers had been in post for up to two years, and only 20 per cent (19) for less than 12 months. However, although approximately ten per cent of nurseries (13) reported having no staff turnover at all during the past two years, the overall picture to emerge was one of fairly high turnover. For example, over a third of the group (34) had lost three or more members of staff and almost a half (44) had lost up to two. Furthermore, almost a quarter of the nurseries had staff vacancies at the time of completing the questionnaire. Given the growing trend of placing babies in nurseries, and assuming that they remain with the nursery until moving on to school, these figures suggest that children will inevitably experience a range of adult carers within the nursery setting. At the present time, the immediate and longer-term effects of this on children are relatively uncharted, and much seems likely to depend on the sensitivity with which nurseries handle the situation with regard to individual children.

Volunteers and students

A third of the nurseries responding to the postal questionnaire reported having at some time had the services of volunteers. Generally these were students or young people seeking experience but parents were also reported as offering voluntary assistance, especially for special events or on outings. A few nurseries reported using volunteers for quite specific tasks: for example, for maintenance jobs, fund-raising, telling stories, playing the piano and giving extra help with children with special needs. However, overall, volunteers did not represent a major resource for any of these nurseries. Notwithstanding this, it was noted that only 20 of the 95 nurseries had developed a written procedure concerning the use of volunteers in their work. One of these 20 was included in the fieldwork phase of the study where it was accorded an 'Excellent' rating on the ERS since it had developed a policy on volunteers which regulated the recruitment, selection, responsibilities, accountability and training of volunteers.

In contrast to the use of volunteers, almost all the nurseries (91 of the 95) had had child care students placed with them during the last three years. Indeed, during our fieldwork visits we became aware that for some nurseries, it was unusual **not** to have at least one student on placement at all times. However, we were rather concerned about the role of students in some nurseries: for example, although students and trainees should be treated as supernumerary in terms of adult:child ratios in the nursery setting, there was a tendency to perceive students as 'another pair of hands', rather than someone requiring support and supervision from staff members. Thus, students were not always closely supervised – on one occasion we observed a student in sole charge of four children in a playroom during an early morning session – and appeared to be allocated an undue quota of the mundane and unpopular jobs (for example, nappy changing). Most child care courses now contain a strong practical element and colleges are finding it increasingly difficult to locate sufficient student placements. It seems likely that it would be in the best interests of all – students (the future workforce), colleges, nursery staff **and** children – if colleges could be more vigilant in monitoring students' placement experiences.

Non-child care staffing

The Children Act Guidance states:

> Each facility should have adequate support staff – for example cooks, cleaners, clerical staff – so that those employed to care for the children are not required to prepare food, carry out other domestic tasks, undertake routine administration or be involved in maintenance of the premises or equipment. (para. 6.41, p.41)

Each of the nurseries in this group of 95 had **some** form of assistance with non-child care tasks, but the degree of assistance varied widely. For example, although a financial contribution was generally required, nurseries in schools, colleges and hospitals often had assistance from staff employed by the 'host' organisation: shared cleaning arrangements were common and nursery meals were quite frequently prepared in the kitchens of the host organisation and transported to the nursery. Only one nursery reported having no cleaner, but laundry was generally undertaken by child care staff.

Almost a third of nurseries in the overall group indicated that they would welcome increased non-child care resources. The most popular request was for improved (or, indeed, simply some) secretarial support, but considerable concern was also expressed about the number of domestic tasks child care workers currently had to undertake.

The development of nursery policy

One of the themes of this chapter has been decision-making and communication within the nursery setting. What is apparent from the foregoing is that having a clear **process** of decision-making is doubly significant for nurseries: their characteristics in terms of, for example, the hours they are open, the shift system, the lack of staff development opportunities and the high levels of part-time staff mean not only that sound systems are of key importance but that they are also more difficult to design. One process by which decision-making and behaviour can be guided is by having clear policies in relation to matters of strategic importance. In recent years both official guidance and codes of good practice have urged nurseries to develop policies in certain key areas. In this section we examine three of these areas: complaints, admission, and safety and accidents.

Complaints

There is now widespread agreement that users of services should have access to a clear procedure for voicing dissatisfaction with services and we addressed this issue in both the postal questionnaire and our site visits. Replies to the former indicated that slightly less than half had a written procedure and most of these reported that this was routinely made available to parents. A number of these nurseries also quoted instances when the complaints procedure had been brought into action and used to successfully resolve a situation. However, 46 of the overall nursery group – just over half – had no written procedure at all and, coincidentally, all the nurseries visited were from this sub-group. From these 15, we gained the impression that such a procedure was deemed to be unnecessary and that, in the main, the atmosphere of the nursery was such that any concerns could be dealt with fairly informally. In four, then, there was a general understanding, amongst the staff at least, that complaints should be channelled to the nursery manager. In the remaining 11 nurseries, even this level of understanding did not exist.

That this situation persists in nurseries today is undoubtedly serious, not simply because it runs counter to the prevailing trend but because it limits the opportunities of parents to have dissatisfaction taken seriously and of nurseries to monitor their practice. Given the wide-ranging day-to-day responsibilities of nursery managers, this may be yet another area to which nursery management committees need to give greater attention. Likewise, it may be that local authority registration and inspection officers could be giving advice and support in this respect.

Admission policy

Having a clear nursery admissions policy has been widely advocated as a means of both ensuring the equitable allocation of places and providing meaningful customer information. In this particular group of nurseries, admission criteria are necessarily complex, given that some places are always tied to arrangements with corporate bodies, such as Midland Bank. In addition, the nature of the arrangement with some of these corporate customers (including Midland Bank) is that they, and not the nursery, are responsible for the allocation of places within their quota. Balancing these factors with the need to take in sufficient income, making efficient use of the existing number of places and being flexible in meeting the changing needs of current users is a skilled management task and one which does not always sit easily with a clear admissions policy.

Although, then, just over half the nurseries responding to the postal questionnaire reported having written admissions policies, these were not always very helpful in terms of describing how places were allocated: in this respect, more informally agreed criteria appeared to come into play. Amongst these, the most significant appeared to be:

- ability to pay the fees;
- priority given to full-time placements;
- priority given to siblings;
- at least one whole day preferred for over-twos;
- a minimum of eight hours per week, spread over at least two days;
- part-time places must 'marry' to make up one full-time place.

Accepting the very real importance of these criteria in terms of managing the nursery, we also attempted to explore the extent to which the individual needs of both parents and children could be taken into account in the allocation of places. The picture to emerge in this respect was very varied although, certainly over the group as a whole, it seemed to be common practice to accord priority to children and families where there was already a sibling attending the nursery. Other priority criteria referred to included: children with special needs or learning difficulties (although at the same time some pointed out that they would not be able to cope with severe disability), social services department referrals (or, in the case of colleges, referrals by the student counsellor or social worker), and lone parents (on whose behalf several nurseries commented that they would like, but were unable, to introduce a special sponsorship scheme).

Furthermore, only three of the nurseries visited were rated 'Good' on the ERS since they had a **written** admissions policy which included equal opportunities considerations. The remaining 12 were each rated somewhere in the range 'Inadequate' to below 'Good', none having a written policy and there being a lack of common understanding of the nursery's practice.

Safety and accidents

Safety is clearly of the utmost importance in an environment where there are young children and aspects of this, as well as health, are both considered more fully in subsequent chapters. Here our aim is to examine how nurseries ensure that safety – as a broad theme – is given the appropriate consideration at all times in the nursery setting. For example, are there clear arrangements for dealing with a range of 'emergency' situations and how are staff kept informed of these?

The postal questionnaire, then, sought to ascertain the extent to which nurseries formally acknowledged the importance of safety in their activities by having written policies. Just over two thirds (64) reported having a written safety policy, almost 60 per cent (56) a health policy and half (49) a written serious accident policy. However, whilst just over one in three (33) had all the above policies available in written form, almost 15 per cent had none.

Several nurseries enclosed copies of these policies which typically covered aspects such as communicable diseases, nappy disposal, administration of medicines, accident procedures, security of the nursery, smoking, fire precautions and procedures, and general hygiene and cleanliness. The format of the documents varied widely, sometimes being intended for staff and thus taking the form of rules and procedures to be followed; in other instances, they were clearly written with a view to assuring parents and it was unclear the extent to which they would actually assist a member of staff faced with an emergency.

Our general view, based on visits to nurseries, was that these nurseries were safety conscious although, as will be seen in later chapters, there are some areas of concern. Ten of the 15 had written policies, although again these varied in the extent to which they provided useful, comprehensive information for staff. Counter-balancing this, five nurseries had no written policy, although in some of these there was a high degree of safety awareness amongst the staff. In one nursery visited for example, within a few minutes of arrival, the researcher was shown the fire alarm and exit, and the procedure in the event of fire explained (this process also being subsequently observed when a group of students visited the nursery). Our overall conclusion, then, insofar as written safety policy is concerned, is that since in operational terms this is a matter mostly affecting staff, policy and procedures need to be clearly set out in a form equivalent to a staff handbook. This would also have the added advantage that in such a form, safety – as a theme – could more readily be incorporated into staff training and staff appraisal.

Discussion

This chapter has drawn attention to the complex task of managing nurseries today. Thus, whilst an encouraging proportion of staff held a child care qualification, in other respects there was evidence of constraints on the extent to which the nurseries were able to incorporate generally-acknowledged principles of good practice.

There appeared, for example, to be quite limited opportunities for staff development and, although it was not the case in each nursery, many nurseries relied heavily on part-time staff. Whilst employing a relatively high proportion of part-time staff has the advantage that such staff can be asked to increase their hours to cover for absences, thereby allowing children some continuity of carer overall, there are also disadvantages. Large numbers of part-time staff may mean frequent changes of carer for children during the day, and a heightened need to ensure that there are infallible systems of communication between staff. The management task overall can also be greater, since the number of individuals a nursery manager is required to supervise and support may produce an unacceptable workload.

Given the introduction of the Children Act, with its emphasis on the need to work with and involve parents in children's care and education, it is perhaps surprising that more priority is not accorded to experience or ability in working with adults when recruiting staff. There are now also heightened expectations of staff in relation to planning children's programmes, and monitoring and recording their progress, and it is disappointing to see how little time appears to be put aside specifically for these tasks on a daily or even weekly basis. A further theme of the Children Act – the need to respect children's language, ethnicity and culture – would perhaps have been expected to lead to the employment of more black nursery staff. It was therefore somewhat disappointing to find that two thirds of the nurseries had a white-only staff group.

The emphasis observed on a team approach to management underlines the flexibility and adaptability required of both individual staff members and the staff group as a whole in today's nurseries. Although at the present time staff appear to be prepared to operate in this way, it may be foolhardy to assume that they always will. Management, therefore, needs to give much greater consideration to staff conditions generally. Our own experience suggests that this is not a matter which all nursery managers have the authority to address. Looking to the longer-term, then, an analysis of management functions in nurseries is indicated and, in particular, the allocation of management roles between nursery managers and management committees.

5. A healthy, safe and welcoming environment for children

As adults, we are all aware of the impact that our physical surroundings can have on how we feel and behave and we tend to take steps to ensure that our environment is as pleasing as possible. Young children, of course, are less able to affect their surroundings and yet it is now recognised that there is an association between the physical environment and children's overall development (Clarke-Stewart, 1982). This chapter, then, looks at the physical resources of the nursery: the premises, the space available and the equipment.

Like Goldschmied and Jackson (1994), however, we agree that a day nursery is a place for **living** as well as learning (in a narrow interpretation of that word) and the environment therefore needs to take account of this dual function: 'it has to combine comfort and homeliness with the practicality of a well run nursery classroom' (p. 16). After describing the physical resources of the nursery, then, this chapter looks at how these resources impact on daily life in the nursery and take account of children's health, safety and general well-being.

The nursery premises

It is a sad reflection on the development of nursery provision in this country that few nurseries operate in purpose-built premises but are much more likely to be situated in an adapted classroom, house or office premises. This was certainly the case for the 15 nurseries involved in the second phase of the research and it would seem realistic to assume that few, if any, of the other 80 nurseries in the sample had the benefit of a purpose-built environment. Our questionnaire coincided with the period during which nurseries were undergoing re-registration and it was therefore a time when some had recently been involved in work to the building in order to meet the space and accommodation standards set by the Guidance to the 1989 Children Act and by their local authority. The re-registration process had also led several to give consideration to what changes they might like to make in the future – and how the cost of this might be met!

General accessibility of the nurseries

As is the case with pre-school services more generally in this country, the development of nursery provision has been such that 'community' provision – in the sense of nurseries which seek to serve fairly well-defined local areas – are relatively rare. For most children and parents, then, a nursery placement involves travel and, as we have indicated already in chapter 3, these nurseries represent no exception. Nonetheless, questionnaire returns from the first stage of the research showed that few nurseries considered their location posed any difficulties for users: only six, for example, suggested that the nursery might not be very easily accessed by public transport. On the other hand, our fieldwork demonstrated the extensive time spent by some children and parents each day in travelling to and from the nursery, with return journey times of more than 90 minutes not being uncommon. For the children of parents who worked full-time – and who still had to travel from the nursery to the workplace – this could mean a very early start to the day and necessitate careful management by nursery and home alike of the child's eating, sleeping and resting patterns.

A further aspect of nursery accessibility which should not be overlooked is the extent to which the needs of those with disabilities are taken into account. Overall, neither the initial survey nor the periods spent on nursery sites suggested that much consideration had been given to this matter. For example, even though one might anticipate that in a nursery pushchair use would raise similar access issues, not all nurseries were fitted with wide double doors or ramps. Likewise, not all nurseries were located in ground floor premises: data from the postal questionnaire suggest that approximately 10 per cent operate from split level sites and, indeed, two of the 15 nurseries visited were based in converted houses, with children being catered for at both ground and first floor levels. Clearly the combination of children and stairs presents issues not only of access, but of safety too. For example, one split level nursery visited relied on a nearby park for outdoor space: consequently, the children had to negotiate the stairs several times daily. A further negative aspect of split level sites noted was the extent to which this arrangement could limit the opportunities for children of different ages to mix together.

Indoor space and its use for children

The wide range of activities which good practice suggests nurseries should offer children necessitates a variety of equipment of different forms and sizes, all of which require space for use and storage. Changing the layout of rooms in the nursery several times in the course of the day is not only very demanding of staff time and energy but also disruptive for children. It is therefore generally acknowledged that the ideal arrangement is having separate areas, permanently available, for activities such as those which are creative and messy, those which involve music or a great deal of space and those for which a calmer, quieter atmosphere is necessary. In Table 5.1 below, the availability of permanent activity areas in the nurseries responding to the postal questionnaire is set out.

Table 5.1   Nurseries with permanent activity areas

Activity areas	No. of nurseries	%
Quiet activity	84	88
Creative/messy	84	88
Large space	69	73
Musical	51	54

Overall, less than half the nurseries (43) were able to provide permanent areas for **all** of these activities, and four were unable to provide **any**. However, the availability of these areas did not appear to be related to either the size of the nursery (in terms of the number of child places available) or to the ownership of the nursery, but more simply to the general limitations of space. Furthermore no nursery suggested that particular activities were withheld for want of a permanent area, although clearly this seems likely to have affected the frequency of some activities.

Maximising the existing space and overcoming space limitations were problems which most nurseries had to deal with, and in the fieldwork phase, we were able to observe the flexibility and imagination staff had brought to this exercise. In two of those visited, space was not a major problem: there were at least six separate well-equipped activity areas (for table activities, water and sand play, a messy area and an undisturbed construction area), organised in such a way that children could make independent use of them and yet still be readily supervised. These received an 'Excellent' rating on the ERS and a further three were rated not far behind with a 'Good' rating. The ten remaining nurseries each had considerable space problems which meant not only that areas had to be dual purpose but that some activities had to be restricted to scheduled times. Quite frequently, too, the dimensions of rooms and the number of children occupying them meant that there were limited opportunities for safe gross motor activity, an important consideration for children attending on a whole-day basis.

Our fieldwork also revealed that although nurseries generally had more than one room available for children's use, the available space and the age range of children on the register often meant that there were only two rooms specifically designated for children (how children were grouped in the nurseries is dealt with in some detail in the next chapter). Using the ERS, we attempted to rate the rooms in relation to their suitability for the groups of children using them. Thirteen of the 15 nurseries were rated as being in the 'Good' range in this respect meaning that rooms appeared to meet the space requirements of the 1989 Children Act and were generally clean, light, warm and well-ventilated. One further nursery was rated as 'Excellent' and another as 'Minimal', the former because, as well as satisfying the 'Good' criteria, the shape of rooms lent themselves to a variety of suitable arrangements of furnishings and equipment. In the case of the nursery with a 'Minimal' rating, there was concern that one of the rooms was dependent on artificial lighting all day, there being no windows to the outside, only on to internal corridors.

We did find in using the ERS that it was easy to overlook some significant features of individual nurseries or rooms. For example, several nurseries were located in pre-fabricated types of buildings, which were subject to extremes of temperature: on the whole staff were vigilant in attending to ventilation (by opening and closing doors and windows) to mitigate these circumstances. However, even these efforts could have limited impact and sometimes bring the additional disadvantage of creating unwelcome outside distractions. Likewise, the exterior walls of many of the nurseries contained a high proportion of glass: whilst the amount of daylight that these provided could be a positive feature, similarly, in the absence of curtains, daylight can become a glare and a strain on young eyes.

Outdoor space for children

Official guidance says very little about outdoor space other than that
it should preferably be adjacent. Arguably, however, the outdoor
space is as important as that indoors. As one set of guidelines for
good practice in group day care (National Children's Bureau, 1991)
puts it:

> A primary difference in indoor from outdoor play is the opportunity to
> exercise in fresh air while developing gross motor control. To this end,
> children need more space to move than indoors, space to run freely and
> pedal wheeled toys actively. Emotionally, children need a place to have
> loud voices without disturbing others. (p.12)

Responses to the postal questionnaire indicated that more than 90
per cent (86) of the overall group had adjoining outdoor playspace
but in some instances it was not **immediately** adjacent. One nursery
had no outdoor playspace at all and made use of park facilities five
minutes walk away. However, although not all nurseries provided
information on the size of the outdoor area, the available information suggests that it was sometimes very limited indeed, dimensions of, for example, 20 feet x 20 feet and 23 feet x 28 feet being cited.

The questionnaire also sought information on the range of
surfaces available on the outside play area and on the availability of
fixed outdoor equipment, such as sandpits, swings and climbing
frames. Not all nurseries replied to these questions but the
information available suggests that most nurseries had both hard
surfaces (such as paving slabs, concrete or tarmac) and grass areas
and several mentioned having additional safety surfaces. Only
slightly more than half the nurseries (49) had fixed outdoor
equipment. In a number of cases without this facility, lack of space,
cost and the threat of vandalism were described as being the main
reasons and in order to compensate for this, several nurseries had
instead decided to invest in portable equipment and wheeled toys.

Overall, the postal questionnaire indicated that few nurseries were
entirely satisfied with the provision that they were able to offer. On
the whole, the deficiencies described related to fairly basic aspects of
the outdoor area: space, surfaces, equipment and storage facilities
but a few nurseries did outline very imaginative ideas for the future
development of the outside area. The rather minimal level of
provision described was generally considered to be attributable to
the relative newness of the nurseries themselves – few had been open
for more than a couple of years – and the decision they had taken to

focus attention and expenditure on indoor developments in the first instance.

The more detailed observation of 15 nurseries confirmed the impression given by questionnaire responses. In most instances, outdoor play areas were not particularly inviting, few representing more than a patch of grass surrounded by a hard area or vice versa. As such, they also provided limited opportunities for children, rather than being an 'outdoor learning area' as described by Goldschmied and Jackson (1994). Not surprisingly, then, the ERS ratings obtained by individual nurseries were not especially encouraging: no nursery achieved the 'Excellent' rating, and although five fell within the 'Good' band, no less than ten of the 15 were rated below 'Good', several at the 'Minimal', or below 'Minimal' level.

Given the full-time nature of the care these nurseries were offering many children, a greater investment in the outdoor area is certainly indicated. Whilst we acknowledge that this would involve additional cost, like Goldschmied and Jackson, we tend to think that staff attitudes may represent as much of a challenge to improvement. Even although our site visits were mainly conducted over the early summer months, we observed some reluctance on the part of staff to use the outdoor area, and when outside, they often tended to adopt a rather passive, overseeing role, not involving themselves directly with the children. Interestingly, too, throughout our observations, we were not aware of children actively seeking to go outside.

Security

The age of children attending nurseries means that the security of the premises, both indoors and outdoors, is vitally important: steps need to be taken to ensure that children cannot leave unnoticed and that only authorised people can gain access to the building or grounds. Questionnaire returns indicated that 59 nurseries employed a door 'entry system', this probably meaning that there was a rule about who could answer the door, rather than that there was an 'entryphone' system in operation. A strong reliance on locked doors, high door handles and staff supervision to ensure that children did not leave the building was also reported. Similarly, a range of different methods was cited as being in use to ensure that children were unable to leave the outdoor area: fences, padlocked gates, lockable gates and constant supervision.

The periods spent on the 15 nursery sites enabled us to assess the effectiveness of these measures in practice and a number of disconcerting situations was observed: main nursery doors which could be opened by an adult and, in one instance, by a child; gates with inadequate or poorly maintained fastenings; low level fencing – and in a couple of instances, no fencing at all – around the outdoor play space. Only two nurseries had proper entryphone systems, whereby all arrivals had to ring the door bell and identify themselves before being admitted – and the effectiveness of these was often quite limited as adults did not always close the door properly behind them. Recent media coverage of instances of day time intrusions to schools has highlighted that security is not a matter for complacency, but one to which all nurseries need to be alert.

Daily living

It is not always easy for us as adults to view situations through children's eyes and, in the case of young children, there are limitations on the extent to which it is possible to ascertain their perspective. This makes it all the more important that adults working with young children continually attempt to evaluate the surroundings and the routines of daily life in order to consider what changes might lead to improvement. In this section, attention is focused on nursery facilities in terms of a range of daily events and activities in which children are involved.

Arriving at the nursery
Because nurseries offer sessional as well as full-time care and attempt to accommodate the time schedules of parents, children are arriving and leaving the premises throughout the day. Generally speaking, however, the busiest times in the nurseries we visited were between 8.30 and 9.30 in the morning, and between 4.00 and 6.00 in the afternoon, the morning periods being particularly busy with parents invariably having further time deadlines to keep. In these circumstances, it can be easy for traffic congestion to build up – both of people and vehicles – and in this respect the provision of adequate and convenient car parking space is vitally important in order both to ensure safety and to avoid the creation of a harassed atmosphere. Responses to our postal survey suggested that the vast majority of nurseries were well-equipped in this respect, 92 of the 95 stating that parents could park their cars safely and conveniently when delivering or collecting children. Our site visits tended to confirm

this, although in a few instances the car parking area was not particularly adjacent to the nursery itself, and in the case of school-based nurseries, a busy playground had sometimes to be negotiated before arriving at the nursery entrance.

Site visits also allowed us to observe the reception facilities in some detail. Few of the nurseries had a specific reception area: more commonly, one entered the main entrance straight into a playroom, where perhaps a table had been set up to hold information for parents to collect and near which a parent noticeboard had been mounted. Aesthetically, these 'areas' had little to commend them and for the child new to the nursery they could be quite baffling, with adults (staff and parents) chatting, and clearly lots of other things going on beyond this among children who had already arrived. On the other hand, observing the arrival of children who had been attending the nursery for some time, it was very apparent how quickly they learned the particular arrival routine of that nursery. Acknowledging the inherent space limitations of most nurseries, our overall conclusion was that the more the reception area could adopt a child-focus, the better for all concerned, not only the children. Ideally this would entail providing a clear floor area of dimensions which would ensure that small children were not caught up in a tangle of adult legs, visually separating the reception area from activity areas, and including an area where children's outdoor clothes and other personal belongings could be stored.

Having said this, all the nurseries visited did attempt to ensure that there were warm greetings and organised departures, despite the constraints imposed by space limitations. Furthermore some form of registration also took place. In one nursery this entailed parents signing children in and out themselves, and noting the times of arrival and departure; this being a system, which if strictly followed, would be of immense value in the event of an emergency evacuation. In most other nurseries, registration was undertaken by staff: in some instances someone was specifically designated to do this, in others it was a question of who was closest and available. Registration procedures were, however, at their most conspicuous at the beginning of the day, and much less evident at subsequent times when part-time children were more likely to be arriving.

Furnishings and equipment for living and learning

As has already been mentioned, most of these nurseries were relatively new and had tended to focus their energies and resources, in the first place at least, on developing the nurseries internally. Perhaps not surprisingly, then, when assessed on the ERS, most of the 15 scored in the 'Good' or above range as far as furnishings and equipment for routine use (eating, sleeping, storage of children's personal belongings) were concerned. In other words, most nurseries were in a generally good state of repair and decoration, had safe and easily maintained floor coverings, and were adequately and appropriately equipped with child-sized tables and chairs.

However, we noted that differences in the physical attributes of individual nurseries could serve to create quite different overall atmospheres. At one end of the spectrum were nurseries where a great deal of attention had gone into the overall decor with toning furnishings, including curtains and furniture, such that the over-riding impression was of a homely, if rather 'smart', domestic environment. Other nurseries had more of a classroom atmosphere: there were no curtains but displays of work stuck to the windows and the furniture, while child-sized, was often rather nondescript and visually unappealing. It did not appear to us that either of these resulting 'environments' was more appropriate than the other. Perhaps, however, nurseries should avoid setting one overall tone and endeavour to create a range of environments throughout the nursery.

Clearly the age and stage of development of the children using the room are important considerations in this respect: babies and children under two have different space and equipment needs from, for example, four-year-olds. The ERS made little direct reference to the provision for the youngest of children (an oversight on our part) and, indeed, we found that several of the nurseries were having to review their arrangements in order to meet the increasing demand for baby places. In most nurseries, a room had been set aside primarily for the use of very young children, sometimes this meaning for children up to the age of 18 months, sometimes up to two years.

Of course, whatever their age, children attending nurseries (especially those attending on a full-day basis) need places where they can rest and sleep. Responses to the postal questionnaire sent to the larger group of nurseries indicated that very few – 18 of the 95 – were in the position of providing a separate room where children could **sleep** during the day. More commonly, older children requiring a nap were transferred to the baby room or a playroom would be used – usually after lunch – as a 'quiet room' for a specific rest period.

A wide range of bed 'furniture' appeared to be made use of including cots, beds, prams, sleep mats, bean bags, canvas beds, travel cots, settees and mattresses.

Furthermore, according to the questionnaire returns, more than two-thirds of the nurseries operated a system whereby each child had their own personal sleeping place. Additionally, the vast majority of nurseries reported it being standard practice for each child to have their own personal bedding. Site visits did not always confirm this: certainly efforts were made to ensure that babies and very young children did not have to share cots or bedding, but this did sometimes occur. As far as older children were concerned much less vigilance was exercised: for example, in at least one nursery, a succession of children was observed to use the same mattress and bedding in the course of the one day.

Sometimes, of course, a nap is not indicated, simply a slowing down of the pace and a more restful period. In this respect, having 'softness' distributed around the nursery in the form of, for example, rugs, cushions and upholstered furniture can create opportunities for children to relax in comfort for a short period. All the nurseries we visited took account of this to some extent but there was considerable variation. This is perhaps best demonstrated by reference to how the nurseries were rated on the ERS which places a strong emphasis on having a **planned** cosy area. Nine of the 15 nurseries had such an area, it sometimes also being the book/reading corner, and two of these were also considered to have 'softness' available in several other areas in the form of cushions, soft toys and so forth. In the case of the remaining six nurseries, there was no planned cosy area. However, with the exception of one nursery where the degree of 'softness' available was considered to be less than adequate, 'softness' was provided in other ways throughout the nursery.

Although most nurseries do have kitchen facilities, these are not always extensive enough for the preparation of meals. This was the case for most of the 15 nurseries which we visited: nurseries located on school, college and hospital sites often relied on the main kitchens of these institutions, and in other instances meals were sometimes brought in from, for example, a nearby residential home for the elderly. As such, there were limitations on the extent to which nursery managers and staff more generally were able to influence both the content of the menu and the presentation of meals. Restricted space also meant that few nurseries were in the position of having an area set aside for mealtimes: in consequence, another area or areas had generally to be adapted each day for this purpose, and space was almost invariably at a premium.

As has already been mentioned, most nurseries had invested in child-sized tables and chairs and, in addition, high chairs were generally available for those who required them. In most nurseries, too, there was an adequate range of appropriate child-safe crockery and cutlery, although this tended to take the form of fairly basic, uninspiring – and often over-used – plastic. On the other hand, we were somewhat concerned by the practice in one nursery of providing toddlers of between 18 and 30 months with no cutlery other than a metal fork, regardless of their ability to use such an implement safely.

Chapter 6 looks more specifically at the 'social' organisation of mealtimes. However as will be apparent from the foregoing, the physical environment of most nurseries – and in particular the limitations of space – tended to do little in terms of facilitating making mealtimes a pleasurable social experience.

Toilet provision is an aspect of the nursery environment which is strictly regulated by the registration Guidelines of the Children Act. However since child-sized fittings enhance independence in young children's use, our postal questionnaire sought to establish to what extent nurseries provided appropriate child-sized facilities in terms of both toilets and washbasins. The replies suggest that the vast majority of nurseries – over 80 per cent – had ensured that all children's toilets were child-sized. Of the remainder, half – almost ten per cent overall – had no child-sized toilets. As far as washbasins were concerned, a more varied picture emerged, with a number of nurseries offering both child and adult-sized facilities and with only two nurseries having **no** child-sized washbasins. Perhaps more disconcerting was the finding that a significant minority of nurseries was inadequately equipped to cater for the needs of wheelchair users, adult or child, with less than two thirds of the nurseries having wheelchair access to at least one toilet.

Responses to the postal questionnaire also indicated that whilst some 25 per cent of nurseries had a separate **nappy changing room**, more commonly a changing unit or changing area had been installed either in the bathroom/toilet area or, where there was a separate baby room, in or adjacent to that room. The majority of nurseries reported having given consideration to the issue of nappy disposal – some employed the services of a nappy disposal company (60 per cent), whilst others used other hygienic methods such as incineration.

However, a small but significant minority appeared to persist in placing reliance on the standard local authority rubbish collection.

Visits to the smaller group of 15 nurseries showed facilities in some nurseries to be inappropriately and inconveniently located such that in some, nappy changing was undertaken in very close proximity to the kitchen, and in a further nursery, older children always had to be accompanied to the toilet. Quite frequently the nappy changing area was rather confined and comprised little more than a shelf for the storage of toiletries, a worktop surface for children to be laid on and an adjacent sink, and there was often a preference for changing older, heavier children on a floor mat. Although in a few nurseries, children had their own personal towel, most nurseries provided paper towel dispensers. During a visit to one such nursery, the towel supply ran out, and all children used the same towel that day. This however seemed to be a rather isolated and extreme instance and overall, the toileting facilities provided by these nurseries would be regarded as acceptable; all, for example, scored 'Good' or above when rated on the ERS.

Equipment

In neither the postal questionnaire nor on site visits was any attempt made to carry out a detailed audit of the range of nursery equipment available to enhance children's learning. Indeed, our observations would support the view (see chapter 2) that how nursery staff encourage children to make use of the available equipment and the accessibility of the equipment are just as significant to their learning as is having an extensive range on hand. Likewise some nurseries appeared to be very well endowed with a range of attractive – and often expensive – brand-name play equipment; whereas in others, a less generous equipment budget meant that the quantity of brand-name equipment was considerably less. However nurseries such as these were often able to provide a range of materials with which children were able to experiment and improvise, either independently or with staff assistance.

The age and stage of development of the children for whom equipment is intended is obviously one of the most important considerations in its selection. Not surprisingly then, this, plus safety, durability and washability comprised the four factors most frequently cited by nursery managers as being the criteria adopted when purchasing equipment. Site visits, however, indicated that nurseries were generally more comfortable in selecting learning equipment for the older age range of children. Thus, although many nurseries had attempted to meet the increasing demand for baby and under-two places by investing in the purchase of new age-appropriate toys, few had taken account of the needs of the youngest of children to explore and investigate through everyday materials and objects. The 'care' as opposed to 'educational' tradition of British nurseries as described in chapter 1 is in no small measure accountable for this. Nevertheless it is encouraging to note the increasing availability of practical advice to childcare workers in this respect (see for example, Goldschmied, 1989; Goldschmied and Hughes, 1992; and Lindon and Lindon, 1993).

From responses to the postal questionnaire it was clear that the limitations of space had meant that most nurseries had had to turn their attention to how to store equipment in such a way that children could still have access to it. A third of the nurseries indicated that they felt they still needed to make improvements in this respect. Our site visits did not suggest that this was a major problem, although in several nurseries the accessibility of some equipment did limit the meaningfulness of 'free-play' time, which effectively was restricted to the use of smaller-sized pieces of equipment and of play materials which had been pre-selected and 'put out' by adults. In this respect, however, we did also observe that much depended on the willingness of individual staff members to cooperate with children's expressed wishes.

Health and safety

The issues of health and safety were discussed in the previous chapter, mainly from the perspective of what policies and procedures existed to guide staff. Furthermore, already in this chapter, reference has been made to a number of specific aspects of health and safety as they have occurred. However, this still leaves outstanding a number of important matters – routine health and hygiene, food and diet and how nurseries deal with emergencies – and it is to these that attention is now turned.

Routine health and hygiene

Hygiene is clearly a very important consideration where numbers of young children are concerned and, overall, most nurseries and their staff were highly conscious of this aspect of their work: hands were frequently washed and disinfectant was in routine use throughout the nursery premises. Additionally, it appears to be common practice nowadays for nurseries to have their own on-site **laundry facilities**: 91 of the 95 nurseries responding to the postal survey had a washing machine, and 90 had a tumble drier also. Indeed, such was the priority accorded this type of facility that, despite the limitations of and competition for space within the nursery, almost two thirds of those with washing machines had a designated laundry room. In others a 'laundry area' had been created somewhere in the nursery, occasionally this being in the kitchen which was not always ideal.

More specifically, the preparation of baby food requires high standards of hygiene. Responses to the postal questionnaire indicate that nurseries were very mindful of this, and for this reason approximately half required the parents to provide ready-prepared food and milk for babies. Likewise over two thirds (69) had also set aside a separate room or area for the preparation of baby food and milk and, in several, a fridge was especially reserved for baby provisions. On visits to nurseries, we observed the regular and frequent sterilisation of baby equipment and toys.

The spread of AIDS/HIV over recent years has focused attention on the need for vigilance in hygiene when dealing with body fluids. Responses to the postal questionnaire suggest that the majority of nurseries now make disposable gloves available for dealing with such situations. However we noted – and had our attention drawn to the fact – that although gloves might be provided for staff, they did not necessarily use them. Questioning staff regarding this, we were left with the clear impression that gloves were seen as a protection for staff, and there was little recognition that children, too, were in need of protection. This certainly highlights the need for nursery staff to be better informed about AIDS/HIV. It is worth noting in this respect that, although five nurseries responded to the questionnaire by stating that **all** staff had had some form of AIDS/HIV training, half of the total group indicated that **no** staff had had any such training.

Finally, the general risks to health associated with smoking are now widely recognised and publicised. In recognition of this, smoking was totally banned in most (88) of the nurseries in the sample. In the remaining seven nurseries, it was restricted to certain designated areas, where children were not present.

Food and diet

In recognition of children's nutritional needs, all registered nurseries are entitled to a milk allowance of one third of a pint of milk per child per day, the cost of this being reclaimed in arrears from the Department of Health. Postal questionnaire responses suggest that the majority of the nurseries (79) took advantage of this benefit, although 16 appeared not to do so, and it can only be assumed that they were unaware of the entitlement. The postal survey also indicated it was standard practice for nurseries to provide a cooked midday meal as well as a mid-morning snack and/or breakfast, and a mid-afternoon snack and/or tea. However, whilst snacks were often prepared on the premises, it was more common for the cooked mid-day meal to be brought into the nursery ready for serving. Thus, although some nursery managers commented that they were able to advise the establishment providing the meals on appropriate menus, these were generally planned by the suppliers and nurseries were rarely aware of what the meal would comprise until it arrived. There was little choice, then, for children and the food was very adult-orientated, the main customers of the providers being adults.

The duration of our visits to the nurseries meant that it was not possible to make a detailed assessment of the nutritional value of the meals offered: however, the relative absence of fresh fruit and vegetables was noted, as was the fact that in most nurseries any special dietary requirements – such as vegetarianism – had to be by special arrangement or organised by the parents. These features – and the lack of choice available – are reflected in the relatively low ratings most nurseries were given on the ERS, whereby only three of the 15 attained a 'Good' or above grading.

Furthermore, although questionnaire responses indicated that the majority of nurseries both maintained a daily record of the food served (85) and informed parents of the menu (84), we saw little evidence of this in practice. With regard to the latter, if parents are to ensure a well-balanced diet for their children, they surely need to be aware of what is being provided at the nursery, and ideally in advance. Also, given the full-time nature of the provision many nurseries now offer, it seems strange that the requirements in relation to recording menus and so forth, applying to establishments offering residential care, do not also apply to nurseries.

Record of drugs given and the administration of medicine

As a general rule, the taking of medication requires monitoring and this is even more the case where young children are concerned. In most nurseries (85), then, a record was maintained of any drugs given. However, the anxiety which this subject can engender in nurseries was evident in the quite complex procedures some had developed for recording. For example, whilst all that was required in 36 nurseries was for the member of staff administering the medication to complete and sign the record, in others the signature of the nursery manager or other senior staff member – or even additional signatures – could be required. Somewhat surprisingly, however, only 17 nurseries reported the requirement that parents be shown and asked to sign the record. Mindful, too, of the fact that ten nurseries reported keeping no record at all, it would seem that a nationally prescribed procedure might be of benefit to all concerned.

Questionnaire responses indicate that practice in relation to the **administration of medicine** is similarly very varied. For example, three nurseries stated they would not administer medicine at all; a further 78 required written parental consent before doing this, and even then would only administer medically prescribed medicines, not palliatives bought over the chemist's counter, while a further 14 indicated that they did not consider written permission from parents as being necessary.

Accidents and first aid

In contrast, nurseries' approach to accidents appeared to be much more standard, with each of the 95 nurseries in the sample reporting that they kept an accident record book, where the circumstances of the accident and the action taken were recorded. It was also reported that this record was shown to parents on their next visit to the nursery and in most instances, the parent was asked to countersign the record, as evidence that they had been kept informed. During our visits to nurseries, we saw this procedure in action on many occasions and observed that it was used for even very minor accidents. It is useful to note in this context, too, that with only two exceptions, nurseries indicated that they were familiar with their own local authority's policy and procedures in relation to child protection.

Minor accidents are, of course, commonplace amongst young children and all nurseries must have a First Aid box or kit available, the precise number of these being dependent on the size and layout of the nursery. It was interesting to note, then, that whilst almost 20 per cent of the nurseries had three or more first aid kits on the premises, almost half (46) had only one. However, the location of first aid facilities is as much part of their availability as is the number and, whilst it is appropriate to keep first aid equipment out of the reach of children, it needs to be readily available to staff at sites where accidents are most likely to occur. Somewhat ironically, then, most first aid boxes or kits were said to be located in the office or the staff room, locations to which children are not normally allowed access.

Fire safety

The age and level of understanding of children attending nurseries makes them particularly vulnerable in the event of an outbreak of fire. Not surprisingly, then, half the nurseries (48) responding to the postal survey reported having had to take action on specific recommendations made by the local fire department. Furthermore, all except three nurseries reported carrying out regular fire drills and, although there was quite a variation in the frequency of these, most appeared to have drills every two or three months and some much more often than this. On the other hand, a few nurseries reported six month intervals between drills; one that there had been 'two drills in two years', and one that there had been no drill for almost 18 months. Given, also, that three nurseries did not have regular fire drills, it may be that clearer national guidelines are indicated. (The National Children's Bureau Guidelines, 1991, recommend monthly fire drills.)

Discussion

Whilst it would be foolhardy to argue that the physical environment of the nursery totally dictates the quality of experiences children have, there can be little doubt that it does play an important role, not only in terms of general atmosphere and comfort, but also in relation to the extent it enables the promotion of children's independence and extends their learning. What we have seen in this chapter, then, is how nursery staff attempt to make the nursery a healthy, safe and welcoming environment for children in a situation where the premises were not designed or constructed with children's needs in mind.

Space, for example, was a major issue for most nurseries but with flexibility and adaptability staff had ensured a reasonable standard for children indoors by compromising on what was available for themselves and parents. The outdoor facilities, however, left much more to be desired and it would appear that as well as increased capital resources, changes in thinking and practice will be necessary if considerable improvement is to be achieved.

There is also scope for improvement in the facilities available to meet children's daily living requirements. Mealtime arrangements, in particular, appear to require further consideration as the combination of spacial constraints and dependence on off-site catering all too often meant that the main mealtime provided limited opportunities for a convivial social atmosphere. Likewise, it was apparent that not all nurseries were best prepared to meet the current demand for baby places, their response to this demand having been restricted to making minor building alterations and purchasing brand-name toys and equipment.

The chapter has also highlighted a number of health and safety issues: the problems posed by split level sites, the need for greater vigilance in exercising fire drills, awareness of safety in relation to HIV/AIDS and the possible need for clarification of procedures and practice in relation to the administration of medication and the recording of food and any drugs provided. However, most importantly, nurseries generally need to give much more attention and priority to the issue of security. Whilst this will undoubtedly have cost implications, the importance of safety and security is such that the need for improvement should not be blurred by financial considerations.

6. Nurturing children's development I
The social organisation of the nursery

Meeting the wide range of young children's developmental needs is both a powerful and challenging responsibility which nursery staff share with the parents of the children attending their nursery. How nurseries fulfil this role is the theme of this and the next two chapters. This chapter examines what we have described as the social organisation of the nursery: how both children and adults are grouped, and the way in which experiences, events and activities are organised within the nursery setting. In particular, the chapter explores how children are grouped in the nursery; the adult/child ratios in use; whether there are arrangements for creating and sustaining significant adult:child relationships and aspects of the nurseries' curricula.

Grouping children

Responses to the postal questionnaire highlighted that children tend to be grouped by age for the major part of the nursery day. Within this broad rule of thumb, however, a few nurseries commented that an individual child's level of ability/stage of development and the occasional need for small work or activity groups could lead to variation. Also, 24 nurseries pointed out that they adopted the 'family grouping' approach for at least part of the day: for example, in one nursery babies joined the older children for tea and for 'circle time'; whilst in another the children were in 'family groups' for meals but otherwise in age-related groups.

Similar variations were evident in the nurseries we visited. The most common arrangement was for the nursery to have two room groupings: the 'baby room' accommodated children from six months (occasionally four months) to two years, and children between two and five years comprised a separate group. However, there were also a few instances of nurseries comprising three groups: in one such arrangement, 'babies' were children up to the age of 18 months, 'toddlers' between 18 and 30 months, and children over 30 months comprised a 'pre-school' group; whilst in another, 'babies' included children up to the age of two years, 'toddlers' were children between two and three years, and three to five-year-olds formed the 'pre-school' group. Only one nursery had four groupings at the time of our visit: 'babies' were children up to 14 months, there were two 'toddler' groups – 14 months to two years and two to three years – and a 'pre-fives' group of children between three and five years. In a further two nurseries, there was no such formalised age grouping of children: children or staff selected groups for different activities – sometimes resulting in children of similar ages being together, and sometimes ages being mixed. Also, as was the case with nurseries responding to the postal questionnaire, several of those visited adopted a system of mixed age groupings or 'family groupings' at meal and/or snack times.

Professional child care thinking tends to argue that whilst there are advantages to children being grouped by age and stage of development, this should not be at the expense of having the opportunity to mix with children of different ages to themselves. However, in the main, our observations suggest that the system of age grouping adopted by individual nurseries tended to be determined by what was possible within the constraints of the spacial dimensions and physical layout of the nursery premises – and the number of children of different ages attending the nursery. As will be apparent from the foregoing, this could mean there being as much as three years between children in the older age group of children, resulting in the potential for a very wide range of levels and stages of individual development within the group. Likewise, the definition of 'baby' employed invariably meant that children of very different needs and abilities would be treated as a group, sometimes with very limited opportunities for mixing with over twos. For example, in one of the nurseries visited, the baby facilities were on a quite separate site from those for older children and therefore the two groups never mixed. However, in another nursery, the babies spent most of their day in the same room as all the other older children, an arrangement which seems likely to pose difficulties in taking account of the individual developmental needs of such young children. Whilst how children are grouped in the nursery may not be of major significance to those children who attend on a limited part-time basis, for those who attend on a full-time, five-day a week basis, nurseries' grouping arrangements will have a considerable influence on the range and quality of their experiences.

Adult:child ratios

With the implementation of the 1989 Children Act in October 1991, new staff:child ratios were recommended, these being: one adult to every three children under two years; one adult to every four children aged between two and three years, and one adult for every eight children aged between three and five years. The Guidance accompanying the Act further states that in nurseries offering more than 20 places, the manager or officer-in-charge must be considered supernumerary, and that in some circumstances – such as when there are very young babies (under 12 months) in the nursery – higher ratios may be appropriate. These ratios were, of course, intended to set minimum standards and local authorities have powers to modify the ratios upwards where they consider it appropriate.

As will be clear from the discussion of how children are grouped in the nursery, few of the sample grouped children in a manner which was directly comparable with recommended adult:child ratios. The postal questionnaire, however, asked nurseries to provide information on the ratios applying in their nursery and Table 6.1 summarises the replies.

Such information demonstrates that in practice staff ratios are not always in line with recommended levels insofar as younger children – those under three-years-old – are concerned. Indeed, less favourable ratios appeared to operate in two nurseries in relation to under-twos and in 31 nurseries in relation to children aged between two and three years. On the other hand, in more than half the nurseries (52) a ratio better than that required by the Guidance appeared to apply for children aged three to five years. It is unclear why there should be such inconsistencies but the groupings used by the nurseries and special circumstances relating to the use of untrained staff may offer at least a partial explanation. In addition, we would again draw attention to our observation that students on placement not infrequently appeared to be used as an 'extra pair of hands' within the baby room of some nurseries.

Table 6.1   Ratios of staff to children

Age band	Ratio	No. of nurseries
Under 2s	1:2	14
	1:3	78
	1:4	2
2–3s	1:2	3
	1:3	6
	1:4	53
	1:5	26
	1:6	5
3–5s	1:2	1
	1:4	5
	1:5	35
	1:6	11
	1:8	38

Totals do not add up to 95 since some nurseries returned incomplete information

Indeed, generally speaking, our observations suggest that whilst most nurseries aspired to conforming with the recommended adult: child ratios at all times, few were actually able to do so. Factors such as the changing number of children attending the nursery each session and staff absences (on account of holidays, sickness, attendance at meetings and so forth) could make maintaining specific ratios a complex task, not always made more straightforward by the operation of a shift system. Replying to the postal question-naire, 45 per cent of the nurseries (43) stated they 'always' managed to maintain the appropriate ratios; 51 per cent (49) that they did so 'most of the time'; and two that they did so '50 per cent of the time'. Interestingly, however, only one nursery confidently claimed to have 'the correct number of staff to cover sickness and holidays'. Although the strategies adopted in order to keep up staff numbers varied, a common approach involved asking part-time staff to increase their hours or full-time staff to work overtime. In addition, despite the requirement of the Children Act Guidance that man-agerial staff should be supernumerary, eight nurseries volunteered that the officer-in-charge or deputy was used to provide cover, a course we also observed when visiting nurseries.

It would certainly be inappropriate to suggest that adult:child ratios are the ultimate measure of quality in nurseries, there being a number of other issues of equal, if not greater, importance. Likewise, the difficulty of **always** having the correspondingly appropriate number of staff for the age distribution and group size of the child population of the nursery should not be under-estimated, not least because the staff costs involved need to be covered. Nonetheless, our observations suggest that nurseries (and inspecting local authorities) may be adopting a somewhat casual approach to recommended adult:child ratios, an approach in which the very youngest of nursery children and those attending on a full-time basis appear to be most at risk of disadvantage.

The key/primary worker system

Stability and continuity – aspects of children's need for emotional security – are known to be key factors in children's all-round development (see for example, Hennessy and others, 1992). However, despite this knowledge, previous research on group care in this country (Ferri and others, 1981 and Marshall, 1982) has shown that in some day care environments children can be denied the benefits of a personal relationship with an adult, the social organisation of the facility being such that the opportunities to have the close and undivided attention of one adult are very limited. In order to address this issue, the introduction of a key worker system – a system whereby every child (and parent) has a 'special' relationship with one particular nursery worker – has been widely advocated (see, for example, Department of Education and Science, 1990; National Children's Bureau, 1991, and Goldschmied and Jackson, 1994). Indeed, in its operational guidelines for nurseries with whom it has a partnership arrangement, the Midland Bank recommends that the key worker approach be adopted.

Replying to the question on the postal questionnaire asking whether or not the nursery operated a key worker system, almost a quarter (25) stated that they did not, preferring instead to base their work on 'more of a team approach'. A respondent from one such nursery also added that since theirs was a small nursery – with minimal turnover in children and staff – 'the children and staff are all very close – we don't need to have things like a key worker system'.

The replies of the 70 nurseries employing a key worker system indicated that having a key worker was considered as being particularly important for babies and for newcomers to the nursery. Several nurseries also chose to emphasise that being a key worker did not mean being the child's sole carer, and again the importance ascribed to working as a team was stressed. Some of the typical descriptions given of a key worker's responsibilities were:

having responsibility for the overall care of the individual children in a group;

developing a special personal relationship with both the children in the group and their parents;

providing security and continuity;

welcoming children and parents to the nursery, being available for discussion, and planning activities for the children.

In addition, in some nurseries monitoring and charting children's developmental progress was described as part of the responsibility of the key worker.

Whilst the above quotations hint at there being subtle differences in how nurseries interpret the key worker's role, the fieldwork visits to 15 nurseries highlighted how marked these differences could be. This situation is perhaps best demonstrated by contrasting arrangements in nurseries which did not see themselves as providing a key worker sysem with those who considered that they did. For example, five of the 15 nurseries visited were amongst those who, in replying to the postal questionnaire, stated that they did not make use of a key worker arrangement and, on the whole, this situation was borne out by our observation. However, having said this, the effects of the arrangements which such nurseries did have in place did not always appear to be markedly different from those achieved by nurseries which stated that they did operate a key worker system. For instance, staff in non-key worker nurseries emphasised, as they did in the postal questionnaire, the high priority they placed on team work, this concept generally meaning that it was considered to be a joint responsibility of team members to get to know all children and their needs equally well. However, in some cases, team membership clearly meant membership of a **room** team, the room comprising a relatively small group of children and an even smaller number of adults. In one such nursery, the two to three-year-olds in the toddler room were divided into two groups, each having two members of staff assigned to it. In this type of arrangement, then, workers knew the individual children in the group very well and, likewise, they were significant people to the children. Arguably, too, there was certainly potential for these workers to be more of a key worker to the children in the group than was the case in two of the ten nurseries which described themselves as operating a key worker system. Notwithstanding duty rotas, the key worker's role in these nurseries was largely confined to greeting the child and his/her parent and saying goodbye in the evening.

Furthermore, even amongst the remaining eight nurseries stated to be organised to take acount of the key worker concept there were wide variations in arrangements. For example, our observations suggest that in only one nursery did key workers take on all of the following responsibilities: welcoming and saying goodbye to children; having meals with key children; undertaking routine 'care' tasks, such as toileting, as well as being involved in play and other creative activities; linking with parents, and assessing, planning for and writing reports on individual children. In one nursery, for example, although key workers sat at the same table as their key children at mealtimes and were responsible for maintaining the children's records and linking with parents, they could be located in a different room for the major part of the nursery day, thus having minimal opportunities for the personal involvement with children which is so central to forming relationships. By the same token, a child could spend the day in the company of more than six different adults, none of whom might have any specific responsibilities regarding that particular child.

As with the arrangements nurseries had for grouping children, whether or not, and to what extent, nurseries operated a key worker system is perhaps most significant in terms of how it impacts on children who attend nursery on a full-time basis. This particular research was not designed in order to pass detailed comment in this respect. However, given the current trend towards full-day care and the importance of stability and continuity in relationships to young children's development, the need for an 'unpacking' of the key worker concept and a more rigorous examination of its imple- mention in practice is clearly indicated. Furthermore, our fieldwork evidence appears to suggest that some practitioners may have an antipathy to keyworking, as shown by the consistent references to a preference for a team approach. Should this be the case, in overcoming such resistance it will first be important to identify and acknowledge the underlying reasons: a process in which further research seems likely to be important.

The curriculum – the nursery programme in broad concept

Over recent years a great deal has been said and written about the early years curriculum and, alongside nationwide debates on the content of the curriculum in compulsory education, the subject has become 'mystified' insofar as many day care practitioners are concerned. Our own interpretation of 'curriculum' is deliberately wide, encompassing all that is said to and done with children, the range of activities and experiences the nursery provides. In this chapter, with its emphasis on the social organisation of the nursery, we look at the curriculum from a particular perspective, considering how nurseries plan for and encourage children's learning, how children's learning and development is monitored, looking at routine aspects of the daily programme and how the nursery links with the local community.

How nurseries plan for and encourage children's learning

Although this topic is not ideally examined by means of a postal questionnaire, the opportunity was taken in the postal survey to begin to explore it. Perhaps not surprisingly, given the British context, all responses placed a strong emphasis on play. In the detail beyond this, however, there was rather less uniformity. For example, some replies referred to the structure of the nursery day, incorporating times for free play, periods for more formal pre-school work and specialised activities like cooking or outings. One nursery specifically referred to the need to obtain a balance between adult-led activities, guided work and free play; whilst another suggested that planning could be too rigid, and hence not allow for children's own preferences. Several nurseries mentioned the planning function of staff meetings, of room team meetings and the role of the key worker in planning for a particular group of children, and in some nurseries use was made of weekly rotas and activity timetables. Likewise a few nurseries remarked on the involvement of parents in the planning process, and others the role of the children themselves in contributing ideas and developing the plans in directions which particularly interested them. A small number of replies – some 15 per cent – alluded to the role of observation (of both groups and individuals) and of records in ensuring a 'plan for play' which met individual and group needs.

On the whole, nurseries were considerably more forthcoming in relation to how they encouraged children's learning. For example, virtually all described how they made use of topics and themes around which other activities were then arranged, some of these themes lasting a term or even longer if children's interest was sustained. Similarly, although very few nurseries referred to using schemas (a technique employed in early years education involving individual patterns of play), most nurseries described how they used a variety of types of play, and different play areas. The following responses give some flavour of nurseries' descriptions of how they encouraged children's learning:

> By offering a wide daily variety with some input from staff but letting children take the leading role in how the activity develops.

> Encourage the children to learn through play.

> ... systematic moving on step by step, moving children forward.

> We treat children as individuals and encourage their interest to learn through varied and creative programmes.

> Providing a wide variety of experiences. Theme work with lots of talking and listening to children. Make learning fun with no pressure.

Generally speaking, these findings were borne out by our observations on site visits: play, comprising periods of both free play and adult-directed activity, constituted the major part of the daily programme. However the extent to which this programme was structured and planned and the balance between free play and adult-directed activity varied widely. For example, although in most nurseries there was a generally observed outline daily 'timetable', in a few there was no such format, meal and snack times representing the only regular daily landmarks. Furthermore, in those rooms or nurseries with a daily programme, we observed a great deal of flexibility in terms of both the extent to which the programme was observed, and the degree of planning which went into it on a daily basis. Indeed, quite frequently, there would be a hurried discussion amongst staff about what they were going to do with the children as, in the absence of planning, no preparatory work had been undertaken. Likewise, in some nurseries there were quite distinct periods for both structured, adult-directed activities and free play, whereas in others the day seemed to be very unstructured, with the children being primarily involved in free play, interspersed with episodes of adult-direction. In addition, staff members had their own individual styles, some being very directional (even in children's free play), whereas other staff took a much more observational stance, appearing to move at children's pace, creating and developing opportunities to extend their experiences and learning. Even within the one nursery, then, children's experiences could vary depending on the staff member involved.

The questionnaire responses and our own observations showed that planning programmes for individual children was not standard practice in these nurseries. Responding to the postal survey, almost half the nurseries (40) replied that they did not undertake individual planning and 20 that this activity was confined to cases where the child was perceived as having a 'problem', such as a learning difficulty or other special need, for which outside consultation or help might be required. This suggests, then, that individual planning – as a formal exercise – was practised in approximately only a third of nurseries. Interestingly, too, in completing the questionnaire, only one nursery wrote:

> No two children are at the same level and so each child has an individual programme so that they can develop at their own rate.

It did, however, appear to us from observation that whilst it might be rare for nurseries to have a formal structure of planning for individual children, at a less formal level – and perhaps without using the vocabulary of planning – some workers did plan for individual children. One such worker, describing a three-year-old we had been observing, stated:

> She's been here for about six months now and about a fortnight ago I noticed she wasn't really ever getting involved in anything – do you know what I mean? – she sort of flitted about – seemed to get bored easily and never quite settled down to anything. I'm not saying she was a problem – she didn't get upset or anything like that, annoy the other kids. Anyway, one day I thought I'm going to see what makes this little girl tick and I kept involving her, asking her questions, making comments. The response was amazing – you've seen for yourself – now she's in the middle of everything, always interested.

At the same time, however, it has to be said that we encountered some staff – trained, as well as unqualified – who, to put it bluntly, appeared to go about their work with their eyes closed, their knowledge and understanding of the children with whom they worked

being quite negligible. An albeit extreme example of this was another worker who described the same three-year-old in the following
manner:

> She's fine – no problem. Her mother works at ... and I think she used
> to go to a minder but I think the minder's given up or something.

Monitoring children's learning and development

Clearly, meeting the needs of individual children is only enhanced
when their learning and development is monitored and we were
therefore interested to explore nursery practice in charting children's progress. In this respect, questionnaire returns revealed that
less than three quarters of nurseries maintained a written record of
individual children's development. One of the 25 nurseries for
whom keeping records on children was not part of mainstream practice volunteered they did not do so because 'labelling' children early
in life was dangerous; whilst another stated:

> If I was seriously concerned about the development of a child I would
> monitor him or her.

Site visits confirmed that not all nurseries monitor and record
children's development and, if anything, this exercise suggested
such practice was even less commonplace than was implied by the
postal questionnaire. For example, on the ERS, only six of the 15
nurseries were rated as 'Good' or better, each of these keeping
records of emergency, health and family information as well as
'profiles' (or other types of developmental assessment records) of
children's progress. A wide range of formats was used for this latter
exercise: daily diaries of children's activities, sleep and eating
patterns; a record of the main developmental milestones; files and
folders containing each child's work; regular reports or reviews once
or twice a year, and developmental checklists of various types.
Examination of these records in the course of site visits revealed that
they were not always up-to-date (in a few, there had clearly been an
effort to redress this prior to our visit). Furthermore, even within the
same nursery, there were marked differences between staff in the
priority they appeared to assign to maintaining such records. For
example, in one of the nurseries visited – said to operate a key worker
system and where the nursery manager certainly placed a strong
emphasis on individual assessment – the records of one worker
(responsible for six children) were so out of date that the file of one

child who had been attending the nursery for more than 18 months contained nothing but blank forms.

The questionnaire data revealed variation in practice in the extent to which the monitoring of progress was undertaken both with the active participation of the children themselves, and in consultation with their parents. Insofar as the former are concerned, the most common practice was relatively informal, observing children in play, listening to them and noting their preferences. However, some nurseries reported that older children were shown their charts and actively involved in their completion and a further nursery reported encouraging children to look through their folders and to discuss how their work had progressed. On the other hand, a more formal approach was adoped by some nurseries who, for example, replied:

Children are requested to do various tasks.

Children produce work for evaluation.

Setting tasks/games as directed from checklist. Care! Child must not feel a failure if the tasks are not attained.

For the most part, parents' involvement in the assessment of children's progress was confined to discussion of the conclusions of nursery staff, rather than an active involvement in the assessment process itself. There were, however, a few exceptions to this where parents were encouraged to adopt a more active role, for example:

Parents are encouraged to discuss all areas of development and to look in folders and at developmental sheets.

Parents can be present during assessments and assessments are discussed with them.

Only one of the 15 nurseries we visited worked with parents in this way.

No matter what format is adopted, and who is involved in the process and how, individual monitoring is a rather pointless activity unless used to inform further work with individual children. Few of the nurseries responding to the postal questionnaire gave a clear indication of how they made use of the assessment records they kept. Overall our impression was that, whilst nurseries felt they ought to assess children and maintain records, they saw no immediate value in this for themselves other than the identification of areas in which children had **not** reached specific developmental milestones. This impression was further confirmed by our more detailed observation in 15 nurseries. This also revealed that many staff view assessing children and maintaining a record of developmental progress as somewhat of 'a chore', and there were consequent differences in the degree of thoroughness with which they approached the task. Most importantly, we saw little evidence of staff making use of the assessments they did undertake to inform their further work with individual children.

Such observations suggest nurseries have not moved significantly from their traditional 'caring' role. A particularly disconcerting feature of this situation is that, even although increasing numbers of children are now spending considerable proportions of their childhood within the nursery, many staff persist in failing to recognise the impact they have on individual children's development. However, as well as bringing benefits to the individual children assessed, the assessment process has other advantages too: it allows staff to examine the values which underlie their expectations and beliefs about children, thus enabling them to clarify the ethos they wish for their nursery, and to develop and evaluate their practice and provision accordingly (see, for example, Drummond, Rouse and Pugh, 1992). As with the concept of the key worker system, then, there would appear to be a need for nursery staff to have improved access to training and developmental opportunities concerning assessment and record-keeping.

Routine aspects of the daily programme

With young children, all aspects of living present opportunities for development and therefore children's experiences of, for example, arrival and departure, meal times, rest periods and their personal care are all as much integral parts of the curriculum provided as more learning-orientated activities. How nurseries organise themselves in these respects is now considered.

Arrival and departure   Notwithstanding the physical constraints of most of the nursery premises we visited, nursery staff placed a high priority on ensuring that there were warm greetings and organised departures for children. On the ERS, only one nursery was rated as less than 'Good', the remainder all having some system whereby at least one member of the nursery staff was available to welcome and say goodbye to individual children. Indeed, seven nurseries were rated 'Excellent' on the ERS since parents, as well as children, were greeted and involved in conversation, and the opportunity taken to pass on any information.

Lunch times   The one absolutely fixed point in the day in all the nurseries visited was lunchtime. Detailed preparations were often necessary, not least because there was no specific dining area and tables had to be cleared and laid, children had to be toileted and seated, ready for the arrival of the food. Invariably an atmosphere of panic and rush pervaded the nursery at this time, with staff trying to settle children, dispense food and converse with children simultaneously – often in very cramped space. A few nurseries managed to calm the atmosphere by having no staff breaks during this period and allowing plenty of time for all the necessary preparations to be completed. For example, children were seated at the lunch table five or ten minutes before the food was due to arrive and this time was then used to sing songs or rhymes, or as an opportunity to discuss what had been happening earlier in the day or, alternatively, what would happen in the afternoon session.

In some nurseries, staff did not sit at the table, eating with the children, and in a few others, whilst they sat at the table, they ate different food. Both these practices seem to be rather questionable, and in the context of residential care would be strongly criticised. In contrast, several nurseries used meal times – and certainly lunch time – to arrange children and staff in tables of family groups. As well as enabling children and their key worker to spend some time together, this arrangement was intended to provide the older children with the opportunity to assist the younger ones and to stimulate conversation. The arrangement was not always completely successful: the key worker might, for example, have to feed a baby or child in a highchair as well as deal with perhaps four or five other children, all in very cramped noisy conditions – not conducive to an atmosphere of calm and intimacy. The degree to which meal times were used as an opportunity to develop skills in terms of using implements, setting tables, pouring and serving varied tremendously: whilst older children were often encouraged to assist with the laying of tables and clearing away, very often meals were served up away from the table by nursery staff and then taken to children.

On the whole, the nutritional value of main meals and snacks was acceptable (although fresh fruit was conspicuous by its absence in several nurseries). Also, in the main, children were gently encouraged to experiment with food they were unfamiliar with or which they said they disliked. Indeed, the only occasions on which we witnessed food being withheld involved pudding being refused until such time as the main course was finished. However, in the vast majority of nurseries visited, the meals provided offered very little cultural variety or choice.

In contrast, with the exception of two of the 15 nurseries visited, a great deal of thought and time was devoted to baby feeding patterns. For example, hygiene and nutritional value were given a high priority, as were parents' wishes. Furthermore, babies were held and talked to while being bottle fed and the feeding of solid foods took place within a framework of pleasant adult-child interaction. On the whole, baby feeding was a popular activity amongst nursery staff and, if anything, this sometimes meant that the task was shared by too many people, and the opportunities provided by the feeding routine for children to form a relationship with one adult could be overlooked.

Post-prandial calm   Whilst lunch itself might be a rather rushed and hectic affair, most nursery routines incorporated a quiet period after lunch. In one nursery, this period was as long as almost 90 minutes with all children – including the older ones – being expected to sleep. In another, all babies and toddlers were put in prams to sleep and placed outside, apparently in all weathers. More commonly, however, the duration of this period was rather more flexible such that individual children's needs – and parental wishes – could be accommodated and children had the choice of being involved in quiet activities, resting or sleeping. In one nursery, the restricted facilities meant that cots had to be located in the main playroom. In most nurseries, however, babies and younger children tended to be moved to the baby room at this stage, where their backs would be gently rubbed or they might be encouraged to relax with a book or cuddly toy. At these times, good ventilation tended to be maintained – although the room might be darkened – and sufficient staff were at hand to ensure effective supervision. Insofar as the older children were concerned, some nurseries actively encouraged certain types of activities such as jigsaws at this stage; in others, the children were free to choose from a wider range of the nursery's equipment for quiet play and, although supervised, there was limited adult involvement.

Personal care and sharing responsibilities   In addition to promoting health and hygiene, encouraging children to participate in their own personal care promotes their self-image and independence. In the majority of the nurseries visited, there was a routine for personal care which involved washing hands before meals and after toileting, which whilst always supervised, also encouraged the development of independent skills. However, although personal toothbrushes were available in a few nurseries, tooth cleaning and hair brushing were rarely component parts of the personal care routine of the nursery. To take account of the vagaries of the weather and for use in the event of accidents, most nurseries maintained a supply of extra clothes and outdoor wear. However, in one nursery all children were changed into 'nursery clothes' each day on arrival at the nursery. According to the staff, 'parents preferred it this way' since it meant the children could return home in their own clean clothes. Raising as it does issues of respect for the individual and of choice, it is perhaps not surprising that some children clearly disliked this arrangement and objected to the choice of clothes made for them. At the same time, in one of the other nurseries visited, the staff positively attempted to develop children's self concept by ensuring that each child had their own face flannel, towel, apron for water and messy play and so forth.

Clearing up more generally, such as after meals, after activities and when engaged in personal care can encourage children's sense of responsibility. On the whole our site visits showed that children were generally encouraged to undertake these tasks and were appropriately assisted by staff. Very rarely, however, was any effort made to explain to children why they were expected to do this – for example to ensure that equipment was left in a suitable condition for the next person. Indeed, what motivated staff to enlist children's assistance in clearing up was quite frequently the constraints of space, and, in particular, the need to clear the floor.

Whilst, then, it would be quite erroneous to suggest that nursery routines took priority over children's needs, these findings do show that nurseries do not always maximise the opportunities – created by routine aspects of daily life – to extend children's learning. In this respect, the nursery premises were not always as helpful as they might be and, in most instances, increased opportunities for staff to review how the daily routine was organised would very likely lead to greater awareness of possibilities.

The wider community

Child-rearing practices throughout time and whatever their cultural base have each had their own – largely informal – methods of introducing children to the concept of the wider community and it therefore seemed appropriate to explore how nurseries deal with this.

Accordingly, various aspects of the nurseries' involvement in their local community was examined both by the postal questionnaire and during our fieldwork visits.

Insofar as taking children out into the community was concerned, the questionnaire data is most clear in terms of major outings. For example, it appeared to be standard practice for the majority of nurseries to have an annual outing to the seaside or some other place of interest and, quite often this also included parents. However, the range and frequency of more local outings was considerably more varied. Roughly similar proportions of nurseries, for instance, reported outings occurring daily, weekly or 'frequently', whereas a similar proportion stated they occurred 'as often as possible'. On the whole, such visits were confined to places within walking distance, only 33 nurseries having access to transport suitable for taking groups of children. Examples of the type of local outings made included: taking children to the park, local farm, post office, bank, library, theatre, hospital, dentist, zoo, aquarium, beach, fire station, ambulance station, pet shop, travel agency; and activities such as swimming, shopping and going on nature rambles were mentioned. In addition, two thirds of the nurseries reported arranging visits to the nursery by people working in the community, such as the police, fire brigade and dental hygienist with most of these reporting at least one such visit in the course of the last 12 months.

Our site visits confirmed the impression given in the survey that promoting children's awareness of the community was not a particularly high priority of nurseries. Indeed, rated on the ERS, only one nursery received an 'Excellent' rating. In this particular nursery, all the adults involved – staff and parents – were made aware of the nursery's aim of introducing children to the community and in fulfilling this aim, many opportunities were provided for the children. In half the remainder, outside visits were comparatively rare and visitors were not invited to the nursery, whilst in the remainder, some priority was accorded to this dimension of nursery life: community representatives, such as firefighters and postal workers were invited to the nursery and, likewise, the children were quite frequently taken on walks in small groups to visit local shops or, for example, to post letters.

An important aspect of how individual nurseries link with the community is whether, and to what extent, they prepare children for the move to their future school. Both our site visits and responses to the postal questionnaire suggest that the wide catchment areas covered by these nurseries makes this a very difficult area of activity. Indeed, less than 20 per cent (18) reported on the questionnaire that they were able to do this and others commented, for example:

> We encourage parents to view this as their responsibility.

> Some private schools don't encourage this.

This is not to suggest, however, that nurseries did not recognise the importance of preparing children for the transition to school and several gave examples of what they did do, acknowledging that it was less than they thought appropriate. For example, some reported attempting to support parents over this period and either sending the child's records on to the school or writing a letter for the parent to take to the school. Others held information about local schools for parents to consult. Quite reasonably, some nurseries stated that their introductory work had to be restricted to those children who would be moving to a very local school, or 'if it was requested by a parent'. In a few instances, there was a standing arrangement for the local reception class to visit the nursery from time to time, and, in some, the local reception teacher or head of primary visited the nursery to make contact with children before school entry.

Discussion

Underlying the topics covered by this chapter are two broad themes. The first of these concerns the extent to which the organisation of the nursery – the format of the day, staff practices and how children are grouped – is such as to promote and extend children's learning and development. The second relates to the degree to which nurseries – as a form of **group** care – take into account **individual** children's needs.

Insofar as the former is concerned, it is quite apparent that in our sample the level of 'performance' covers a very wide range from 'less than adequate' to 'excellent'. Nonetheless, it is worth pointing out that few nurseries could be described as uniformly 'good' or 'bad': more commonly they tended to be excellent in some respects, whilst in others there was certainly scope for improvement. Similarly, in relation to the second theme, whilst we observed that some staff members were exceptionally good at working with individual children, some were not: indeed, even when a nursery received a poor rating on the ERS, we witnessed individual instances of good practice (and, of course, vice versa). However, what is perhaps most disconcerting is the limited extent to which acknowledged good practices – such as the key worker system, planning and individual monitoring – have been incorporated into nursery policy and how they have been implemented. There was often a poor understanding of the benefits of these practices, suggesting the need for their greater promotion and development of such ideas. Nonetheless, having said this, it is doubtful whether such a responsibility should rest with the nurseries themselves: indeed, the case for greater **public** investment in this respect is strongly indicated, this being a theme which is taken up in the final chapter.

7. Nurturing children's development II
Activities and experiences

The focus of this chapter is the way in which nurseries nurture all aspects of young children's development: their physical development, the acquisition of cognitive and language skills and their personal and social development. As modern textbooks on child development underline, however, the foregoing aspects are not discrete and activities designed to meet one type of development can provide opportunities for supporting learning in other respects. For instance, whilst an activity might be primarily geared towards gross motor skills, it is also likely to present learning opportunities in relation to communication and social skills such as the use of language and turn-taking. Likewise, each of the areas of children's development is responsive to a range of learning modes – free play, exploration, adult-directed activity, small groups, large groups and so forth – each of which provides opportunities to promote, reinforce and extend the child's learning. This chapter begins, then, by examining how nurseries balance group time and free play and the responsiveness of adults in these periods. It then moves on to look at the work nurseries undertake in each of the areas of children's development and given, as discussed in the previous chapter, that it is now widely recognised that children's overall development is influenced by their feeling of emotional security and well-being, we begin with that aspect. As with previous chapters, the data on which the chapter is based come from both the postal survey and fieldwork visits to 15 nurseries, although here there is a greater emphasis on the latter.

Group time, free play and adult responsiveness

One of the purposes of our site visits was to examine the balance between group-time (adult-directed activity) and free play (children's choice) and to examine the roles adopted by adults in such sessions. However, as discussed in the previous chapter, a great deal of flexibility appeared to exist even when an outline daily programme had been produced, and the reasons for this were not entirely straightforward: sometimes inadequate planning and preparation was the main factor (invariably caused by there not being **scheduled** planning time); at other times the mood and wishes of the children required an alteration to the programme and, sometimes, the style of individual workers meant that what was intended to be a free play session took on the form of a more adult-directed activity. In addition, whilst the wide age range of children accommodated in a nursery room often indicated making extensive use of small activity groups, the limitations of the nursery premises often made this very difficult to achieve. In consequence, then, there are constraints on the extent to which it is possible to draw general conclusions about nursery practice in this respect.

Nonetheless, what is appropriate to note is that none of the nurseries visited kept children together as one large group for all of the nursery day: each provided periods of free play as well as more organised adult-led group activities. However, in three nurseries, very little time appeared to be given over to **planned** group activities – either in one large group or a number of smaller ones – and in the resulting 'free time', the adults' role appeared to be primarily that of a supervisor of, for example, safety and behaviour. Such nurseries were rated as less than 'Good' on the ERS. A wide range of practices was observed in the remaining 12 nurseries but each of these did provide children with opportunities to be in both relatively small groups as well as larger ones in the course of the nursery day. In seven of these 12 nurseries, the change in group size was part of a conscious decision by nursery staff to add variety and to change the pace throughout the day and in four, rated as 'Excellent' on the ERS, free play and small groups tended to predominate.

Insofar as free play itself was concerned, all the nurseries had large and varied supplies of play equipment to suit most ages of young children, although the limitations of space generally meant that access to some of it was restricted. Likewise, in each of these nurseries, free play sessions were scheduled to occur regularly at least once a day. However, it was in the staff involvement in these sessions that most variation was noted, and sometimes such was the variation within the nursery that it was impossible to speak of a **nursery** style. As mentioned earlier, for example, some staff seemed to consider their role in these sessions as supervisory only, intervening to modify behaviour and being watchful of safety considerations. Notwithstanding the importance of these matters, other staff became more involved with the children and their play, attaching an educational value to their involvement, albeit sometimes of a fairly directional nature with little regard to children's need to explore independently. The following observation in one nursery demonstrates the different styles of two adults: one staff member is supervision-oriented, engaging in few interactions with the children other than to control them, whilst the other tends to take positive moves to avoid conflicts and to facilitate learning, sometimes by observing the child but allowing him/her to explore alone and at other times, engaging the child in one-to one or other small group activity:

At the beginning of the observation only one staff member (SM 1) was on duty, looking after a group of 11 children aged between 30 months and almost five years involved in free play. Two of these were in the book corner, one looking at a book (A) and the other lying on a bean bag playing with some small toy figures of both people and animals (B). The remaining nine children were all sitting on a large mat, playing in an assortment of fairly loosely formed groups with building equipment and with cars. SM 1 sat on the edge of the group and immediately in front of her two four+ year olds were energetically racing and crashing cars (C and D), watched over by the youngest member of the group (E). SM 1's eyes constantly moved round the group but she did not speak. E gets up and starts to walk amongst the older children towards the back of the room to some toys:

SM 1: Be careful, E, don't trip up. Where are you going?
(E carries on, finds a toy car larger than those played with by C and D and starts to come back.)
SM 1: What are you going to do with that E – are you bringing it here?
(E nods and continues. Arriving back at C and D, E looks hesitantly at what the other boys are doing and slowly tries to find his place back on the mat. He pushes his car into one of the other cars.)
C: No don't do that it's too big (E stops for a moment and then starts again).

Then:
C: No don't (taking the car away from E; E looks rather petulant)
SM 1 : That's enough, C – he only wants to play. Give it back to him.
(SM 2 arrives back in the room and surveys the scene.) She says:
SM 2: What have you got E – a car? Come and let me see your car (SM

2 sits down on the mat near the home corner, E moves towards her)

SM 1: Yes you go and play over there. (E arrives at SM 2)

SM 2: Oh it's a red car, C. isn't it? (E nods and starts to push the car along the ground).

SM 2: Where is the red car going E? Is it going to the shops? Or is it going for petrol?

E: Petrol. (E moves the car around in circles). Where's the petrol? (E keeps moving the car; A moves over and SM 2 pats her knee, indicating for A to sit on it. A sits on SM 2's knee and watches E.)

SM 2: Do you think you've gone past the garage E?

A: I see the garage – it's here. (E moves to A)

A: I'll put the petrol in (mimes putting petrol in, E copies) – it needs lots of petrol – then it will go a long, long way. Now we can go (imitates sound of moving car and both children crawl across the mat, making car noises, making the car negotiate hills and corners, round and over other children's toys. SM 2 remains where she is – she watches A and E together and silently listens and watches B on the bean bag. Totally absorbed, B is moving the animals around in his own purposeful way, but the moving contours of the beanbag mean that the figures often topple over. E and A approach with the car).

SM 2: Oh look you're coming to a farm – can you see the animals? You'll have to go slowly now.

A: (Waving) We can see the animals. It's a farm.

SM 2: Are you the farmer B ?

B: No – I'm just playing with the animals.

SM 2: (to A, B and E) We know a song about the animals on the farm, don't we. Will we sing the song?

B: No – the story.

SM 2: OK – can you find me the story, B – what book is it in – do you remember?

(B goes to the bookshelves and looks for the book; A and E join in; E gets rather excited and starts pulling the books out in a rather haphazard manner and throwing them on the floor.)

SM 1: We don't throw books, do we E? Put them back on the shelf.

A: I've found it – this one.

SM 2: Well done A . OK – let's put these books back first and then we'll have the story. Does anyone else want a story? (The three children and SM 2 start to put the books back; three other children come and join the small group – several pile on to the bean bag – SM 2 beckons to E to sit beside her, she puts her arm round his shoulder so he can see the pictures – the animal story begins...)

The role of nursery staff in balancing children's need to explore independently and pursuing opportunities to extend learning is one which relies not only on skilful judgement but also on a knowledge of and familiarity with individual children and their particular stage of development. In this respect, and as a general rule, the individual differences between staff made it difficult to give **meaningful** ratings to nurseries on the ERS. However, whilst the research did not attempt to look systematically at staff interactions with children at different developmental stages, we did have some reservations about nursery practice in relation to the very youngest of children, and in particular babies.

This is not to deny the popularity of babies among staff generally nor the substantial investment in equipment and adaptation to premises that many nurseries had made in order to meet the increasing demand for baby places. However, very often this investment appeared to have been made with more attention being given to the physical aspects of the premises and health and safety matters generally than to children's developmental needs. For example, even when a key worker system was in operation, the key worker was often responsible for several very young children and thus reliant on other staff for assistance at opportune times such as feeding and changing. Indeed, we have already commented on the fact that students were quite frequently used for tasks such as nappy changing. Furthermore, not all nurseries operated a key worker system, or a key worker system whereby key worker and child were actually in the same room for the major part of the day. Likewise, much of the equipment purchased, whilst visually attractive and conforming to safety standards, presented rather bland opportunities to assist very young children's sense of discovery and concentration. To take just one example: in recent years, the concept of 'the treasure basket' has been advocated for group day care situations (see for example, Goldschmied and Jackson, 1994) as a means of introducing variety and quality in infant play. The basket contains a variety of objects – none is plastic, none is a 'bought toy' and many are in everyday use – which offer interest through touch, smell, taste, sound and sight. Somewhat surprisingly, only one of the nurseries visited was making any attempt to make use of this concept, and even then the basket contained objects comprised primarily of plastic.

Given the high proportion of their waking hours that young children may be spending in the nursery setting, it is particularly important that nurseries make use of all existing knowledge about what is beneficial to children. It may well be that the recent, relatively sudden increase in demand for places for babies has taken nurseries rather off-guard, and that improvements in practice will automatically follow in the fullness of time. However, knowledge of the importance of the very early years suggests that a high priority should be given to facilitating nurseries in this process.

Personal development, dealing with emotions and making relationships

A range of factors contribute to children's social and emotional development and in the previous chapter, a number of these such as how children are grouped in the nursery, whether they have a significant adult to whom they can relate and so forth, were discussed within the context of the social organisation of the nursery. Another such factor is having a positive sense of self and of self-worth and early years commentators suggest that adults working with young children need to consider having an overall strategy which actively values **all** children (see, for example, Lindon 1993).

Valuing all children

A practical aspect of valuing all children entails providing them with opportunities to see adults to whom they can personally relate – the kind of adult they might be when they grow up – and the adult world therefore needs to provide positive images of both sexes, of different ethnic and cultural heritages, of different skin colours and of a range of abilities. In the postal questionnaire, and on fieldwork visits, we explored nurseries' anti-discriminatory practice.

The postal questionnaire specifically asked nurseries to describe how they avoided discrimination in relation to ethnicity and culture, gender and disability. With regard to ethnicity and culture, most nurseries chose to describe their equipment stating that it was multicultural or represented a range of cultures through dolls, jigsaws, dressing-up clothes, play people, books, displays, pictures and other play materials. Only a few nurseries supplemented their description of equipment with accounts of their wider approach to this issue, the following being some such examples:

> We teach children to be proud of their culture, and value other languages.

> Children are not compared to each other in any way. They are all individuals in their own right.

> Children are encouraged to talk about their differences.

Insofar as gender was concerned, the majority of nurseries reported that their approach included ensuring that all activities were available to both boys and girls, as well as encouraging all children to make use of the entire range of equipment. As one nursery put it, 'cooking, brickbuilding and woodwork are available for all'. In this context, too, a few nurseries made reference to paying particular attention to the use of language, being careful not to use stereotypes and to challenge sexist remarks. These same nurseries also reported that they exercised prudence in their selection of books, equipment and posters, ensuring that they did not portray men and women in a stereotypical manner.

The vast majority of nurseries responded to the issue of disability and anti-discriminatory practice by stating that they would attempt to avoid turning a child away from the nursery on account of their disability, but acknowledged that this might only be possible by charging a higher fee. In this context some nurseries also added that, in their view, all children have special needs, and that each – regardless of ability – was treated as an individual. A few nurseries also reported having visits from people with disabilities, and in one case the nursery and a nearby school for children with disabilities had a regular arrangement of reciprocal visits. And, finally, referring to its code of practice, one nursery clarified that no child would ever be excluded from an activity, rather the activity would be adapted to enable the child's participation.

Our visit to one nursery poignantly highlighted the need for those dealing with young children to be alert to the need to deliver positive images of all children, regardless of colour or culture, when a four-year-old Sikh boy volunteered that his skin was dark because he had just been on holiday in Blackpool! Nonetheless, overall our visits to nurseries suggested that providing positive images and avoiding discriminatory practice was an area in which most nurseries had scope for improvement. For example, whilst many of these nurseries had written equal opportunities policies, and some policies on anti-discrimination also, these had quite often been written by the nursery's parent organisation and nursery staff had little 'ownership' of them. Furthermore, we observed little **planned** use of material in such a way that cultural awareness and anti-discriminatory practice could be described as being an integral part of the curriculum. Thus, no less than 13 of the 15 nurseries were rated less than 'Good' in relation to cultural awareness on the ERS, ten of these being at the 'Minimal' or below level. In some of these nurseries what little, if any, attempt there had been to introduce ethnic or cultural diversity was quite minimal with toys, play equipment and pictures tending to depict one ethnic group only or to depict black people in a non-positive manner. In one, for example, whilst the public area of the nursery featured photographs of black people, they were represented in the context of a developing country (man fishing and a woman washing clothes), rather than in positions of authority or in families. Likewise, although several nurseries celebrated a number of religious festivals such as Eid and Chinese New Year, there appeared to be a danger of these being portayed as something rather 'exotic', and it was unclear the extent to which their celebration promoted respect for the culture or religion concerned. Furthermore, in at least one nursery, the celebration of religious festivals was restricted to Easter and Christmas because, according to the manager, 'there are not many multicultural children in the nursery at the moment'.

Insofar as gender was concerned, all nurseries were observed to offer the whole range of activities to both boys and girls. Indeed on several occasions boys were seen in the 'home corner' taking on domestic and caring roles and girls were seen 'being the doctor' and playing with cars. Furthermore, although on one occasion a member of staff was heard to say, 'Now, I want two strong boys to carry that heavy box next door', sexist language was on the whole positively discouraged.

Whilst a number of the nurseries visited mentioned that some children attending had had poor language development when they were first enrolled, very few nurseries were currently working with either exceptionally gifted children or children with special needs. As was the case in responding to the postal questionnaire, the nurseries visited stated that they were open to all children whatever their special needs and, indeed, in four we saw how the nursery environment and programme had been adapted to meet the requirements of individual children. One such example was of a severely epileptic baby who attended a nursery on a part-time basis: this child was passive and needed stimulation (as well as a great deal of sleep) and the nursery was able to adapt the routine and provide the appropriate equipment in order to accommodate the child's physiotherapy sessions. However, given nurseries' funding base and the fact that the needs of some children with disabilities might necessitate additional staff time and thus a higher fee to meet such costs, how 'open' nurseries can be in this respect must be rather doubtful.

Whilst, then, nurseries appeared to be making some progress in terms of their awareness of the need to work in an anti-discriminatory manner, undoubtedly there was still scope for improvement. We ourselves were particularly concerned about the issue of ethnicity: the lack of attention given to this matter by some nurseries in today's multiracial society gives great cause for concern. This is not to deny the complexity of this matter – having an equal opportunities and anti-racist policy, having equipment which represents a range of cultures and having cultural representation on the staff group are all significant **starting points** – they do not, however, guarantee truly anti-discriminatory practice which values all children.

Promoting children's sense of self-esteem

Responses to the postal questionnaire suggested that, more generally, a high priority was placed on promoting individual children's sense of self-esteem and some of the positive and constructive approaches described were as follows:

> Children's efforts are always praised and encouraged.
> We don't make comparisons between children.
> We don't push children to perform.
> Activities are tailored to meet individual needs.
> The uniqueness of each child is recognised.
> Every child is allowed to develop at their own pace.
> We ensure that children are not set up to fail.

Overall, our observations in the 15 nurseries confirmed that nursery staff acknowledged the significance of self-esteem to children's optimal development, although, as with so many other aspects of practice with children, wide differences were noted between individual members of staff. The existence of such variation meant that we did not consider it appropriate to give four nurseries the 'Good' rating on the ERS. Differences within staff groups also contributed to our decision not to rate any nurseries as 'Excellent': in this respect, whilst we did note that some staff, on the basis of their own observations, **targeted** specific children in their giving of praise (or responsibility) and worked through and with parents on this, overall there was insufficient evidence to suggest that such an approach was **common** practice within the nursery.

In the main, however, adult praise for children in these nurseries was realistic and meaningful. For example, in contrast to the type of praise which is rather too general to be meaningful such as 'What a lovely painting ... what a pretty dress', we more commonly encountered instances such as the following:

> (to child cutting piece of toast in half):
> Do you need some help? You are trying hard!

> (two-year-old building 'house' with Duplo)
> Child: Look at my house!
> Adult: That's your house is it?
> Child: I making big.
> Adult: You're getting good at that, aren't you...

> (three-year-old doing jigsaw)
> Adult: You're doing very, very well there, B. That's the first time you've done that one.

> (four-year-old making 'pictures' on board with tap-tap shapes)
> Adult: Did you copy that, D or did you make it up?
> Child: I copied it (shows illustration)
> Adult: You are brilliant, D. Well done!

As with 'praise', staff also tended to adopt a positive approach in reminding children about rules and behaviour, in commenting on achievements, and in enlisting children's assistance in communal activities. For example, it was rather unusual to hear nursery staff say 'Don't (run)' but instead they would say 'We always (walk, because...)'. Likewise in commenting on achievements, the emphasis was not solely on the completed task or in drawing attention to what had not been done but on encouraging on to the next stage.

Help in understanding and expressing emotions
Healthy social and emotional development encompasses learning to recognise and express feelings. In their replies to the postal questionnaire, only a few nurseries reported being other than satisfied with their practice in this respect and described the following approaches as being standard:

- physical contact and comfort;
- individual one-to-one attention;
- use of expressive equipment and materials – role play, puppets, sand;
- acknowledging 'It's OK to feel angry/sad';

- encourage children not to suppress emotions but to talk about how they feel;
- use of nursery pets;
- liaison with parents.

Our observation in nurseries highlighted many instances where staff reacted very sensitively to children's need to express and understand feelings, one instance being when an adult commented to a wandering rather unsettled child, 'Are you alright, N – you look a bit sad today?' In response, the child nodded agreement and went off to play, apparently more content. Here again though, there tended to be considerable differences between members of the same staff group. On the whole, however, it did appear that the base from which most staff were operating derived more from a 'caring for individual children' perspective than from one which placed importance on raising children's general awareness in this respect. For example, acknowledging that the periods of our visits were relatively brief, we did note that opportunities presented during activities such as story-telling to explore feelings – 'sadness', 'anger' and 'happiness' – were often missed. Whilst this approach seems likely to be attributable to the traditional 'care' training of day nursery staff, the example highlights the potential value of an approach more geared to children's developmental needs.

Setting boundaries and limits

The setting (and maintaining) of boundaries and limits – discipline – is one facet of guiding young children's behaviour and their social development and, quite clearly in this respect, adults must not only be consistent in their approach but also ensure that what they convey is disapproval of the behaviour, not dislike of the child concerned. Responses to the postal questionnaire showed the majority of nurseries feeling that they handled this aspect of practice well and, on the whole, this was borne out by our nursery visits. For example, 11 of the 15 were rated 'Good' or above on the ERS, this meaning that staff were generally consistent in the limits they set; acceptable social behaviour was encouraged by praise ('It's nice to hear you saying thank you'); by the staff themselves providing models of considerate attitudes to others; and by quickly identifying and dealing with unacceptable behaviour, involving parents where this was persistent. Indeed, in several of these nurseries recent examples were cited of difficult and persistent behaviour, such as biting, where a home/nursery strategy had been agreed between the parents and staff. In the four nurseries rated below 'Good' on the ERS (two of them at 'Minimal'), the differences in approach of individual staff members was considerable and with some displaying a very 'controlling' approach, the overall rating of the nursery had to be reduced despite the good practice of most staff.

Space to be alone

Whilst one of the benefits of attending a form of group pre-school provision is the opportunities thus afforded for social contact with peers, young children also need to be able to spend time alone – or perhaps with just one other child – in relative privacy. In two of the nurseries visited, the limited space and consequent arrangement of equipment and furnishings made it virtually impossible for children to find solitary space and, because of this, these nurseries were given a lower than 'Minimal' rating. In a further eight nurseries, space was not specifically set aside for children to be alone, but should they choose to, the children were allowed to find their own space or to create it, for example behind furniture or in play equipment. An illustration of this type of activity was a three-year-old playing near, but not with, another group of children. The supervising adult was aware of the child and what she was doing but did not interrupt in any way as the child chattered animatedly to herself whilst she transported farm animals in a cart between farm and garage.

The five remaining nurseries were rated 'Good' or above in this respect (one of these as 'Excellent'), each having space set aside for one or two children to play, out of sight of other children and protected from intrusion by them. It was characteristic of some of these nurseries not only to allow children to be alone but more actively to encourage this in the sense that play-alone activities were part of the curriculum and used for the development of children's concentration, independence and relaxation.

Opportunities to care for others

Providing children with opportunities to care for others – be these adults, their own peers, children younger than themselves or animals – encourages the development of their sense of responsibility. In the course of our observations, we noted that nurseries fostered such a notion in a number of different ways: for example, they were encouraged to care for the equipment and premises, to leave things ready for the next person to use, and to 'run errands'; the birthdays of children and staff were celebrated and where the nursery adopted a family group arrangement at mealtimes, older children could assist younger ones with feeding, pouring and so on; in some nurseries, the older children took turns to hand out the mid-morning snack and to help lay tables and clear away after meals; and several nurseries kept pets, most commonly a hamster, which the children could help to feed and clean out. However, despite these observed examples, as many as ten of the visited nurseries were rated below 'Good' on the ERS, mainly because this aspect of children's development did not appear to be well-recognised: while children were expected to be sympathetic, this was not facilitated by staff and, likewise, there was not a concerted attempt to facilitate child-child interaction or to help children care effectively for others.

Did the children seem happy? – the overall 'tone' of the nurseries

The ERS used during nursery visits includes a sub-scale 'Tone', which is intended to give a general impression of the quality of the **interactions** within the nursery. However, before describing nurseries' ratings on this scale, we believe it important to clarify that we consider there to be a distinction to be made between interactions and relationships: we may have a pleasing interaction with the person we are standing next to in the bus queue, but it does not therefore follow that we have a relationship with that person. Interactions are nonetheless important, not least because they give some indication of how 'happy' children are and because this general 'tone' is a key constituent in forming an initial impression of the nursery for both parents and children alike.

In this respect, then, four nurseries were rated at less than 'Good', this being because there was a significant proportion of the staff who tended to be rather inattentive and unresponsive to children, often becoming involved only when problems arose. Whilst it would be misleading to describe the resulting atmosphere as tense, neither could it be described as relaxed, and unsmiling faces and loud voices were quite frequently encountered. In contrast, in the 11 nurseries rated as 'Good' or above, a calm, but busy, atmosphere pervaded and the children mostly appeared to be very happy and relaxed. Cheerful voices and smiling faces – both of children and adults – were also characteristic of these nurseries and the staff tended to show warmth towards the children through physical contact such as gentle holding and hugging. Likewise, in these nurseries the grouping of the children and the arrangement of the nursery day was such that children tended to be with the same children and the same core of staff members for most of each day, facilitating continuity and stability of adult-child and child-child relationships. Indeed eight of these eleven nurseries were rated above 'Good' (and three of these as 'Excellent'). Two factors were particularly significant in this respect: first, for the most part, staff in these nurseries managed to prevent problems occuring or escalating by their use of careful observation and skilful intervention, and, secondly, the 'curriculum' of each included some positive attempt to develop children's social skills, both informally and through stories and discussion groups.

Understanding and using language

As children's verbal communication skills develop, whole new vistas of learning open up: language enables them to respond and initiate communication with others and to develop and understand concepts. For children who attend a nursery, that nursery will be a significant contributor to this aspect of their development.

Children's **understanding** of language is promoted by a range of unplanned everyday activities as well as more planned access to books, storytelling, finger plays and so forth. Each of the nurseries had a reasonably wide selection of books but of course the value of such equipment lies as much with how staff encourage its use as it does with simply having the equipment available. One particular nursery, for example, appeared to 'excel' above all others in instilling in children a love of story telling. Here the collection of books readily accessible to the children was considerable and the children were constantly asking staff to read to them, either individually or in groups. In other nurseries, whilst there tended to be at least one story telling session daily, this was not always totally successful, and sometimes a proportion of the books were held in the office, not generally available to the children. In addition to the skill of the story teller and the choice of story, the success of story telling sessions was affected by a wide range of factors. For example quite frequently, rather than breaking up into small, age related groups, the 'audience' comprised the whole age range of the nursery, and perhaps in excess of 20 children. Holding attention in these circumstances was often extremely difficult and made no easier by virtue of the fact that story telling was often scheduled to coincide with a time when other activities were being set up or tables cleared:

there could also be constant interruption as children were taken out in ones and twos to the toilet.

However, overall, given that in most nurseries there was an easy, relaxed atmosphere in which talk flowed, and where children and adults generally listened and responded to one another, the majority of nurseries were accorded a 'Good' or above rating on the ERS in relation to receptive language. One of the factors contributing to a higher than 'Good' rating was the use some nurseries made of audio-tapes in encouraging children to listen and identify sounds, and to become familiar with the words of songs and rhymes. In at least three nurseries regular daily use was made of television or videotape – a rather more controversial practice than the use of audiotape. In one of these nurseries, children grouped round the TV mid-morning and again after lunch to watch children's programmes and the television was again switched on at about 4.30 by which time most children had already left this particular nursery. In a second nursery, a videotape was put on after lunch and children watched this when they had finished their meal and been to the cloakroom; whilst in a third, the television was used most days for a children's programme in the early afternoon.

Children's **use** of language may likewise be promoted both formally and informally and, in general, although it was considered that the majority of the nurseries visited were quite competent in this respect, a wide range of skills was observed. For example, some staff members – and this was very much universal practice in two nurseries – exhibited a good understanding of how children's language develops, and in both free play and more organised activities, made particular efforts to encourage and help children to express themselves: by talking about what they were doing, asking open-ended questions, describing and interpreting pictures and jigsaw subjects, playing structured table games, and explaining, recalling and predicting events. Such practice invariably meant that there was not only much open-ended conversation in the room involving many children, but that there were child-child as well as adult-child dialogues. The following extracts from recorded observations illustrate this type of practice:

Group of 4-year olds with water, teapots and so on
C1. Oh, no, look, that one might smash!
C2. Mine won't smash.
A. Why won't it smash?

C2. It's metal.
C1. Mine's plastic.

Group of three and four-year-olds at lunchtime
C1. I'm going to cricket.
A. Is that tonight?
C1. Yes with my daddy
A. I've never been to a cricket match. Have you been before?
C2. I've been – my brother plays – and we watch.
C1. We have tea at the cricket.
A. And do you play?
C1. Sometimes but not at the cricket...
A. Where do you play?
C1. In the garden.
C2. Me too – whoosh!
A. What's that – are you hitting the ball? (C2 nods)
C2. It can go a long way and then you win.
C1. My daddy can hit the ball a long way – then you get six.
C2. Six runs yes – then you win.

At the other end of the spectrum, whilst adults did converse with children, there was a marked tendency to ask questions which invited only short or 'yes/no' replies, and did not always encourage children's talk. Furthermore, in some nurseries a few staff were inclined to limit language to controlling children's behaviour and managing routines, such as getting ready for lunch, clearing up, preparing to go outside, the following being one such example:

Three-year-old involved in a cutting and painting activity
A. Don't tread on the books!
C1. We've got a bag to keep them safe!
A. Do you want to do a painting?
A. Now be careful with those scissors ... keep sitting down.
A. Cut them out nice (sic) and I'll do some glueing later on.
C1. I've got a doll...
A. Right, both arms in together. You go and sit there. No, there.
A. What colour would you like? Red, blue, white ...?
C1. White
A. Bit more on your brush, bit more ... (followed by similar
    conversation with other colours)
    Right, that's enough! Fold it and press down. Keep pressing.
C1. I'll lift it!
A. Not yet, I haven't told you to , have I? Press it down.
C1. Pick it up!
A. No, not yet! ... Right – now! Isn't that beautiful! Go and wash
    your hands straight away. Can you take your apron off?

When dealing with the very youngest of children, the staff in the vast majority of nurseries engaged in much verbal interaction, imitating sounds and chatting, and using gestures and body language to encourage responses from babies. With toddlers, they often repeated what the youngster had said, elaborating or pronouncing, as appropriate, words correctly without being discouraging. Only two of the total 15 nurseries were rated below 'Good' in this respect, in the main because they displayed a tendency to use language primarily to control children's behaviour: in these nurseries, for example, phrases such as 'No, you musn't do that' tended to predominate in verbal interactions. Furthermore, the unfortunate habit we noted in quite a few nurseries of staff having conversations unrelated to the work of the nursery when supposedly working with children was rather more conspicuous in the baby room than elsewhere in the nursery.

Creating and exploring – children's cognitive development

Whether or not day nurseries consider it part of their role, and whether or not they plan for it, there can be little doubt that they contribute to children's cognitive development: the receptiveness of the young mind means that all children's activities and experiences are significant in this respect. Furthermore, given the high proportion of their waking hours that many children spend in the nursery, we would argue that nurseries have a **responsibility** to take cognitive development into account in the range of activities and experiences they provide for children. Since in most nurseries a major part of the day is occupied by what the ERS describes collectively as 'creative activities', we begin by first considering nurseries' approach to these and then discuss how they respond to and encourage children's interest in the wider world.

Creative activities and experiences

On the ERS, creative activities include art, music/movement, sand/water, dramatic/role play, bricks/construction, plastic material (clay, playdough, plasticine and so on) and woodwork. All of the nurseries visited made some provision for each of these activities with the exception of woodwork, which, in ERS terms, was provided by only one nursery. However, only four nurseries had consistently 'Good' or above 'Good' ratings on the ERS for the remaining activities, these also being nurseries which, for the most part, scored better than 'Good' for the balance they achieved in offering these activities in both planned, adult-led groups and on the basis of individual choice. Only one of the remaining 11 nurseries consistently scored below 'Good' across each of the creative activity areas, whilst the others appeared to be very strong in some areas, but particularly weak in others.

Music/movement and sand/water play were the two areas in which the majority of nurseries received higher ERS ratings. Music, mainly in the form of singing, was most frequently available as an organised group activity on a daily basis. One nursery had an excellent range of 'proper' musical instruments but this nursery was exceptional in this respect and, more commonly, taped music was relied on, and often used in association with games such as 'musical chairs' or 'statues'. A further nursery was observed making use of professionally recorded music and movement activities, encouraging listening skills as well as rhythm and movement.

Sand and water play was also available very frequently – usually indoors and often on a daily basis. Both structured and more free play sessions involving water/sand were observed, the former often being linked to the introduction of the concepts of measurement and weight, as in the following example:

> The children were experimenting with water in a small group with a teacher: pouring water from different sizes and types of teapot into cups, seeing how many cups filled each teapot, and how many cups each teapot would fill. The teacher asked questions which elicited concepts of consistency, full/empty, more/less, breakable/unbreakable, and the children developed these to talk about waterfalls and home experiences.

Insofar as art, dramatic and role play, brick and construction kits, and plastic material activities were concerned, a much wider range of practice was noted. For example, whilst most of the 15 nurseries visited (10) had a wide variety of art material available including felt-tip pens and paints as well as more three dimensional equipment such as scrap materials, six were rated less than 'Good' on the ERS, three as 'Good', and six above 'Good'. A feature of those nurseries accorded a higher than 'Good' rating was the particular effort they made to relate children's art activities to other experiences by, for example, encouraging children to paint representations of special experiences, a new baby at home or a trip out. A certain amount of adult-direction was characteristic of art activities in all nurseries to some degree and often appropriate as, for example, when a group of children was involved in painting a large display. Generally, how-ever, adults were responsive and encouraging of children's efforts, ackowledging the value of the activity not only as a form of self-expression but in providing opportunities for conversation and discussion. In contrast, the art activities of two nurseries were considered to be overly adult-directed and thus to provide limited learning opportunities as the following observation describes:

> The Fathers' Day cards had been prepared by an adult, who had drawn a snooker table on each. The children then took it in turns to stick a piece of tissue paper (already rolled into a ball for them) on to a blob of glue put in each corner by the adult. They seemed fairly bored in the process, and no attempt was made to gauge the appropriateness of the snooker table to the fathers concerned or to take account of the needs of children with absent fathers!

Just over half the nurseries were rated as less than 'Good' with regard to both dramatic/role play and plastic materials activities. As far as dramatic/role play was concerned, most nurseries had a reasonable stock of dressing-up clothes and other props (often donated by parents and staff) but difficulty in accessing it and its focus on domestic and household roles meant that its use and value were rather limited. For example, in one nursery all the clothes were stuffed into a tall laundry basket which had to be totally up-ended every time a child wanted something from it. Hangers seemed to be unsatisfactory as items tended to fall off them easily and hooks had three or four items hanging on top of each other, making access difficult for children. To a very considerable degree, then, in most nurseries dramatic/role play was not a spontaneous activity initiated by children without considerable staff encouragement, and likewise not all staff appeared confident in encouraging this aspect of play. Some imaginative work did, however, appear to be undertaken in a small proportion of nurseries by, for example, turning the home corner into a shop, a hairdresser's, a post office, or a cafe. In one nursery we observed how, after an outing to a local cafe, children were helped to set up their own 'cafe' in the nursery, wearing appropriate clothes, using relevant language, serving each other, writing bills and making and using 'money' to pay for their refreshments. In the same nursery, a hairdresser's was set up the following day, and all the children washed each other's hair; in the afternoon the 'salon' became a beauty salon, and children made up each other's faces with face paints. Instances such as this demonstrate how, by providing an activity which builds on a shared experience, nurseries can promote and extend children's learning in a way which is also fun.

As with dressing up clothes and other role play props, modelling materials such as clay, playdough and plasticine tended to be available in all nurseries but their use was rather restricted and more might have been done to make this an activity of interest to children, and thereby one in which learning might be supported. For example, in a few nurseries the range of equipment was restricted to play-dough and plasticine, and the plasticine could be very hard and the colours had become so mixed that it formed an unattractive grey lump – not at all inviting for either its visual or tactile qualities. Although in most nurseries a wider range of materials was available, the limitations of space (a restricted 'messy' area) often meant that these could rarely be offered on a frequent basis. Only one of the 15 nurseries visited was rated as more than 'Good' in this respect, this nursery being accorded an 'Excellent' rating on account of the opportunities it created for children to experiment with different degrees of moisture and dryness, extending this to experimentation of the effect of adding eggs, milk and so forth to a basic material such as flour.

However, the area of creative activities in which the majority of nurseries achieved their least satisfactory rating was in relation to bricks and construction kit material: only three were rated 'Good', one as 'Excellent' and no less than 11 as less than 'Good'. To some extent, the high frequency of low ratings is attributable to the ERS placing a great deal of importance on the nursery, or individual room, having a specially set aside construction area – and this was simply not the case for most of these nurseries. Indeed, most nurseries did have a good supply of bricks of various sizes and a range of small and large construction sets, together with appropriate accessories such as vehicle, people and animal figures. However, despite the fact that some nurseries did attempt to facilitate this aspect of children's play by occasionally rearranging the furniture for a short period, overall, the opportunities for children to make extended use of such equipment were rather restricted. There is no doubting the popularity of play of this type to all ages of children attending nurseries: during free play sessions it was always extensively used. Given this intrinsic interest to children and the fact that such material offers opportunities to extend learning in a number of different areas of development, it seems particularly unfortunate that more is not done to facilitate and maximise its use.

Overall, then, it was not so much the lack of creative activity equipment which accounted for the wide range of ratings on the ERS: but the constraints of the physical layout of the nursery and more especially, the skill, perseverence and, perhaps, inclination of the staff group to overcome these, and to create and, seize opportunities for learning in this respect.

Investigating the wider world

Reference has already been made in this chapter to the varied extent to which individual members of staff appeared to be aware of children's need to learn by exploration, and to be able to assist them in this. Such variation was also apparent when attempting to assess nurseries in this respect, with almost half those visited (7) not succeeding in achieving a 'Good' ERS rating. In nurseries awareness of children's need to explore and investigate was evident but the overall nursery approach was rather ad hoc and there was little evidence of a **planned** programme. In the remaining eight nurseries, there was considerably more evidence of the nurseries attempting to create a range of appropriate experiences to engage children's curiosity of the world around them and in one of these, rated as 'Excellent', the flexible and individualised approach meant that staff responded to children's choice of interest and were able to assist them to move forward at an appropriate pace.

In the previous chapter we discussed the extent to which it appeared to be practice for nurseries to encourage children's awareness of the community: children's learning may also be extended by being provided with opportunities to explore the natural world. For example, the already mentioned activities with natural materials such as sand, water and clay enable children to gain experience of the properties of these substances. In the majority of nurseries visited, encouragement of children's exploration of the natural world was largely limited to such experiences and for this reason, few were rated as 'Good' or above using the ERS, and two were rated at less than 'Minimal'. However, in four nurseries a much wider range of experiences was offered to children. For example, within the confines of the nursery premises, children experienced ordinary garden soil, grew plants (outdoors as well as indoors), 'studied' worms (one nursery had an indoor wormery), tadpoles, stick insects and other 'mini-beasts' and sometimes these activities were supplemented and encouraged by visits to, for example, woods or the sea-shore. In one of the nurseries visited, a staff member had a particular interest in the natural world and on the basis of this had introduced a number of projects on 'growing', as well as a permanent 'nature table'. The contents of this table did change but at the time of our visit it accommodated fish, tadpoles, newts, wormery, gerbil and plants, in addition to nature books open at appropriate pages. This development was, however, dependent on this member of staff and in the majority of nurseries, this breadth of exploration of the natural world was rarely available to the children.

An equally valuable approach to exploration involves building on something in which the children show interest by creating 'interest' areas, perhaps in the form of a wall or table display. For example, an interest shown in a wristwatch might be followed-up with a display of different types of timepieces to which the children could contribute, and with older children this might develop into a discussion of the theme of time or measurement. With younger children, the tactile qualities of a range of different objects might provide a similar focus. Although several nurseries we visited did have wall-mounted 'investigation' displays, these were rarely the focus of current attention and only four had an ongoing 'interest' table. Indeed, when rated on the ERS, only five nurseries achieved a 'Good' or higher rating and several were significantly below the 'Good' level. When asked about the absence of an interest table in one of these latter nurseries, a member of staff replied: 'younger children tend to destroy them.' This statement does highlight the space difficulties experienced by many nurseries, but having said this, it was also the case that other nurseries with similar difficulties did manage to undertake imaginative work in this respect. Two such ongoing projects in the nurseries visited included one with the theme of 'growing' (which included the natural world, with children planting broad bean and sunflower seeds), and another prompted by the discovery of a bird's nest focused on eggs, hatching, the development of feathers and so forth.

Examining individual nurseries' ERS scores in relation to the range of both creative and investigatory activities confirmed our overall impression that it was the same few nurseries which received consistently better scores than the majority of the others. The clear implication of this – assuming our sample is reasonably representative – is that only a few nurseries are proactively attempting to extend children's cognitive development. Whilst this itself is significant, it is all the more so because there appears to be no one particular contributory factor such as the proportion of qualified

undertaken, and much expensive equipment tending to be under-used. One of the underlying reasons for this is undoubtably the cultural shift involved in making the transition from a role in which one 'occupies' children to the more proactive one of pro- moting and extending learning. This is not a straightforward transition to achieve, nor one which can be effected speedily. However, given the important place that nurseries now play in the lives of many of the children who attend them, this challenge is not one which can afford to be ignored.

8. Nurturing children's development III

Parents as stakeholders and partners

Providers of group day care for children have long been encouraged to recognise parents' knowledge and experience of their own children and to work in partnership with them. Indeed, the concept of partnership is now embodied in the Children Act of 1989. 'Partnership' can be said to operate on two levels: at one level, it relates to parents and providers sharing the care of individual children and a strong emphasis is therefore placed on communication and sharing information, thoughts and experiences of the child, in order that the child knows that the adults are 'acting as one'; the other level recognises the contribution that parents as a group are able to make to the total nursery environment in terms of both practice and policy. Both levels are emphasised in the National Children's Bureau guidelines on group day care (1991) which state:

> The nursery should be planned as much as possible as a real partnership with parents/carers and based on understanding how nursery life can complement the home. Parents/carers should be fully informed about the general operation and constraints of the nursery, and they should be welcomed as contributors to the fullest possible extent. (p. 53)

It is also noteworthy that from the outset of its child care scheme, Midland Bank has recommended that there should be parent representation on the nursery steering group or management committee.

The aim of this chapter, then, is to examine partnership in practice. As in previous chapters, the data are drawn from both the postal questionnaire and site observation visits. However, in this instance, these data are supplemented by information from 322 parent-completed questionnaires, as well as by 57 brief interviews with parents receiving subsidised day care. Using the parent questionnaire data, the chapter begins with a profile of the parent-users of the nurseries and how they assess and evaluate day care provision. Parents' satisfaction with the nurseries involved in this research is then explored and, finally, this is followed by a discussion of how nurseries attempt to foster 'partnership' with parents.

Profile of the parent users; how they assess provision

The parent group

The parent questionnaire was randomly distributed to between 15 and 20 parents in each of the nurseries visited (not necessarily Midland Bank employees) and Table 8.1 summarises some aspects of their socio-economic situation. In the main, it was mothers who completed the questionnaire, reflecting the fact that it tends to be women who take responsibility for child care arrangements. In consequence, for at least the 93 per cent of respondents described as being part of a two-parent family, the **Employment situation** refers mainly to female employment, and **Partner's employment** to male employment.

In addition, almost 90 per cent of the parents responding to the questionnaire reported having access to a car during the day, whilst 53 per cent reported being a one-child family and 84 per cent that they had only one child attending the nursery. A high proportion of the parent users of these nurseries might, then, be described as follows:

> Female, white, in a two-parent family, with one child, living in an owner occupied house, having use of a car during the day, employed full-time or part-time, with a partner also in work.

Day care subsidies

As was described in chapter 1, Britain's scant provision of publicly provided day care means that the many parents using 'private' day care tend to have to meet the cost of this themselves. However, many of the nurseries involved in this research, such as those in colleges, universities and hospitals, had been set up to meet the needs of employees and also quite frequently offered subsidised provision. Furthermore, the partnership arrangement which some organisations, such as Midland Bank, had with individual nurseries often included an element of financial subsidy to their employees.

Table 8.1 The socio-economic situation of parent users

Characteristic	%
Housing situation (n = 322)	
Owner-occupied housing	89
Private rented housing	7
Council rented accommodation	4
Totals	100
Employment situation (n = 322)	
Working full-time	39
Working part-time	37
Students	18
Self-employed	3
On maternity leave	3
Career break	1
Totals	100
Partner's employment (n = 301)	
Working full-time	90
Irregular work pattern	6
Working part-time	3
Students or not working	1
Totals	100
Ethnicity (n = 322)	
White/European	91
Asian	4
African-Caribbean	2
Other	3
Totals	100

Although we did not endeavour to assess the extent of employer-provided financial support experienced by the parents using the nurseries involved in the research, 40 per cent of the 322 parents completing the parent questionnaire reported receiving some degree of subsidy towards the cost of their child's day care. A wide range in the level of subsidy was also reported. For example whilst subsidies of between 30 and 50 per cent were cited by some parents, in colleges and universities an even wider range appeared to operate, with free provision quite frequently being available for students, while staff might receive only a 20p reduction in the hourly rate. It was, however, characteristic of many parent respondents that although they knew what they themselves paid in child care fees, they were rather less aware of the level of subsidy they were receiving, and hence had little idea of the real costs of providing nursery provision. Some parents received their subsidy in the form of Childcare Vouchers and, quite understandably, such parents were highly critical of the fact that in terms of the Inland Revenue the vouchers were seen as a 'perk' and therefore subject to tax.

Brief interviews with 57 parents receiving an employer subsidy enabled us to explore the experience of applying for a subsidised place. From these it appeared that some anxiety and confusion could surround the application process. For example, whether the application was made during the early stage of pregnancy, during maternity leave or when the child was born, confirmation of the place tended to take some time. Parents indicated that a minimum of three months between confirmation and return to work was necessary in order to give themselves and the child time to prepare for the change, but ideally they would prefer to know even earlier (Midland Bank gives confirmation at three months). Whilst these parents did ultimately receive a place and were therefore satisfied, they did recall they would have welcomed rather more feedback during the waiting period rather than, as they described it, 'being kept in the dark'. Furthermore those who had no guarantee of a place until less than eight weeks before returning to work described the whole process of application as 'nerve racking'. These interviews also suggest that as subsidised places are taken up and the demand for nursery places grows, the experience of applying for a subsidised place can become much less straightforward for parents. Two respondents, for example, described the difficulty they encountered when they were unable to obtain a subsidised place for their second child: in one case, the two siblings had to be placed in different nurseries and in the other instance, the mother was giving serious consideration to whether she would return to work after maternity leave. Nonetheless, whilst a few subsidy recipients mentioned that their manager had written a 'business case' in support of their application, none felt they had had to fulfil any particular eligibility criteria.

Respondents, however, left us in little doubt that being able to return to work and receiving subsidised child care had been the optimum outcome for them, as the following comments demonstrate:

> It has all fallen into place ideally for me.

> Couldn't be better...perfection, in fact!

> It's a brilliant scheme – it's time other employers realised the benefits and did the same!

Having said this, however, a substantial number of respondents indicated that had the subsidy not been available, they would have found some other way to continue working, by, for example, employing a nanny (especially where there were two children), finding a childminder or another nursery. About a quarter volunteered that, in the absence of the subsidy, they would probably not have returned to work, especially if they had more than one child.

Deciding what form of child care to use

Theoretically parents are able to choose from a range of different forms of child care: nurseries, nannies and childminders. For many of the parents whose children attended these nurseries, however, the choice was curtailed, not only by what was available and affordable locally, but also by virtue of the fact that they were reliant on the subsidy, and this was generally linked to only one local nursery. For many of the parents, then, it was not so much a case of actively choosing nursery care over other forms of care but that the nursery was part of a more complex set of decisions about returning to work or study and the availability of some form of subsidised child care. Notwithstanding this, most parents – and especially working parents – appeared to feel that nursery care had two outstanding advantages over other forms of day care: first and foremost, as parents, they could rely on it being available, unlike a childminder or nanny who might become ill or suddenly decide they do not want to continue to offer a service; and, secondly, because it offered children a range of social experiences and friendships.

What parents look for in a nursery

Acknowledging that few parents had actively chosen the nursery their child was attending, we nonetheless attempted to gain some insight into what parents consider important by asking them (a) to identify three attributes which they particularly liked about the nursery their child attended and (b) to imagine they were advising a friend on negative things to avoid and positive things to look for in nurseries. Insofar as the former is concerned, Table 8.2 describes the frequency with which the five most commonly cited characteristics occurred.

Table 8.2   Features parents liked about nurseries

Features	No. of parents
Locality/accessibility	215
Qualities of staff	157
Facilities available	131
Fees	75
Reputation/recommendation	67

Although these were the characteristics most frequently cited by parents, this is not to say that they reflect parents' order of priorities. Indeed, a number of other characteristics were quite frequently mentioned and were invariably of prime importance to the parent concerned. These included the fact that the nursery had been 'approved'/provided by an employer; the general atmosphere, and especially the fact that the children appeared happy; the standard/quality of care provided; the management and organisation; the hours of availability, and the availability of part-time places and places for babies; the hours of opening; the size of the nursery; the meals provided; flexibility; and safety/security.

When asked to put themselves in the slightly more objective situation of advising a friend, it became quite apparent that parents rarely have specific criteria in mind when they view a nursery, and tend to be guided by somewhat vague and general impressions, or as some put it 'a gut feeling', arrived at after one quick visit to a nursery. Nonetheless the list of positive features raised by parents in the course of this exercise was very similar to that already described in Table 8.2 except that there was somewhat less of an emphasis placed on the practical aspects of accessibility and fees.

The general categories 'Qualities of staff' and 'Facilities available' again ranked high on this list but being broad categories, they warrant further elaboration. As far as the qualities of staff were concerned, for example, some parents were exclusively concerned about staff numbers and the adult:child ratio. On the other hand, several emphasised the need for staff to be trained and qualified, mature and experienced. Overall, however, it was the **personal** qualities of staff which parents focused on, preferring staff to be a variety of combinations of the following: 'approachable', 'caring', 'competent', 'friendly', 'helpful', 'intelligent', 'kind', 'loving', 'patient', 'sensible', 'sympathetic', 'understanding', 'warm', and 'well organised'.

Under the heading of **facilities available**, the most commonly cited features were the premises themselves (adequate space and outdoor play area as well as being colourful, bright and lively) and having a wide range of quality equipment (including large equipment) and books, all maintained in good condition. Several also mentioned the need for a wide variety and range of stimulating activities and the few parents who differentiated between 'play' and 'education' indicated a strong preference for the inclusion of educational and learning activities. Also mentioned in this context was the desirability of having some structure or routine for the day, although the need for flexibility within this was also raised. Factors much less frequently mentioned included the following: flexibility of hours; partnership with parents; evidence of equal opportunities practice; a welcoming attitude to parents; the grouping of children and the level of interaction and communication.

Asked to describe the features which should be avoided, aspects of staffing and premises were highlighted, with nursery organisation/ routine and safety and security also being very frequently mentioned. The following list gives an outline of the particular issues to which parents ascribed most importance:

- Staff:
  not qualified, insufficient numbers, unloving, lack of care, not supervising, uninterested, harsh attitude, instability/turnover, rigid attitudes, shouting, aloof, unfriendly, domineering, dictatorship, not hugging children.

- Premises:
  no kitchen, cramped space, too plush, too crowded.

- Organisation/routines:
  too regimented, unplanned day, disorganisation, general sloppiness, organised for staff convenience.

- Safety/security:
  not given enough consideration, anyone could come in, lack of supervision of the children.

Sometimes the list produced by a parent had quite a Dickensian flavour to it, as illustrated by the following two responses:

> Strict regime; Frosty atmosphere; Unclean surroundings.

> Children look bored/miserable; Carers ignoring children; Inadequate premises/facilities.

While these different exercises provide some quite consistent messages about the areas to which parents ascribe the greatest importance (and few professionals would argue with these), we were left with the impression that few parents have very clear ideas about what constitutes 'good provision'. Indeed, as some parents themselves pointed out factors such as the nursery being registered with the local authority and being approved for use by an employer, such as Midland Bank, were considered to be all-important assurances of quality.

Some organisations have produced guides to assist parents in making choices about day care (see for example *Choosing Child Care*, 1991). However these are not widely distributed and neither do they have a particular focus on nurseries. More importantly, there appears to be limited advice available to parents in terms of the needs of children in full-day care, and, in particular, the needs of very young children in this respect. Given that parents are well-placed to monitor and influence quality in nurseries, this information gap seems to be a serious omission.

Parents' satisfaction with the current nursery

Parents completing the questionnaire were also asked to rate how satisfied – very satisfied, quite satisfied, fairly satisfied or not at all satisfied – they were with the following aspects of the nursery their child attended:

- the equipment and play materials;
- safety;
- the premises generally;
- the general level of care provided;
- the general level of education provided;
- the extent to which they, as a parent, were made welcome by the nursery staff;

- the extent to which they were kept informed and consulted in relation to their child;
- general level of parental involvement;
- days and hours of provision and fees.

In drawing conclusions from parents' views on the quality of care their child is receiving, an important consideration to bear in mind is that few of these parents have much scope to choose between nurseries. This being the case, unless they are seriously dissatisfied, they are unlikely to 'vote with their feet' and move their child elsewhere. Furthermore, as has been shown in situations where social services departments attempt to deregister provision, parents often develop a certain loyalty to 'their' nursery and are resistant to criticism of it.

Perhaps not surprisingly, then, the 322 parents completing the questionnaire appeared to be a contented group, for the most part being 'very satisfied' with the provision offered. However, notwithstanding the **overall** level of satisfaction expressed, there were three areas about which a certain degree of concern was consistently expressed. These three areas were: fees, the premises, and, as a parent, being kept informed.

Fees

A number of issues were raised in relation to fees but most frequently it was concern about the high level of fees which was expressed, a number of parents making the general point that subsidies (from government or employers) should be much more widely available. The fee structure of some nurseries was also a source of dissatisfaction, parents feeling that they were having to pay for time they did not use because, rather than charging by the hour, nurseries charged by the session, or even by the day. Likewise parents, such as teachers – who were at times liable to pay a retainer fee – tended to be critical of this practice. In one sense, these concerns reflect the fact that parents are not necessarily aware of the true costs of running a nursery. On the other hand, whilst many parents took the opportunity of completing the questionnaire to point out that they could afford the nursery only because of an employer subsidy or because both parents were earning good salaries, several also commented that they would rather pay more for good care than accept lower standards.

Premises

The concern about premises came largely from the parent users of seven particular nurseries and reflect issues raised by our own observations. For example, parents tended to refer to both the suitability and size of the outdoor play area and to the security of the nursery.

Being kept informed

Here, it was not so much that parents were actively dissatisfied but that they expressed a preference for a slightly different approach. For example, although there was generally positive feedback from parents on the welcome they received at the nursery and on the information given about the day's events, several indicated that they would welcome having the occasional, more formal reporting of their child's progress. Likewise, several parents expressed the view that they would find it helpful if nurseries informed them of positive achievements, rather than initiating discussions about problems only. Two apposite comments in this respect were:

> (I) would appreciate more feedback on general behaviour, inter-actions, moods, and so on – with both the good and the bad.

> To us parents 'little things' that they do or new words they say are 'very big things' to us.

Overall, then, the limited concerns which parents did have about the nurseries did not relate to how they met the needs of children. Indeed, in this respect high levels of satisfaction were reported, and any additional comments which parents did make were within the context of 'further improving existing good practice'. For example, each of the following positive suggestions was made by parents who had otherwise described themselves as 'very satisfied' with that particular aspect of provision:

> There could be more discussion about personal safety. Indoor climbing equipment should be available for wet days and they could have less ambitious topics, which lasted for longer.

> They could provide a bit more pre-school activities as a preparation for reading and writing.

> Extra stimuli could be provided for 3-5s – possibly a part-time teacher.

> The external premises aren't very good. Playground surface could be relaid.

Fostering partnership

The foregoing sections provide some insight into parents' expectations of nursery provision but to what extent do nurseries make a
positive effort to facilitate partnership? Utilising data from the
postal questionnaire and site observations, this section considers
how nurseries introduce parents to their facility, what methods are
used to ensure communication with parents, and how parents can
become involved in the overall running and management of
nurseries.

Introducing parents to the nursery

Relationships can be strongly influenced by first impressions and in
this respect it is interesting to note that the vast majority of nurseries
responding to the postal questionnaire had taken the step of producing a leaflet or prospectus for parents. This was given to parents
either at the time of their initial enquiry or when the child began
attending, and in terms of format, length, and content could vary
considerably from nursery to nursery. For example, some were
expensively produced, clearly set out booklets or handbooks, others
were in the form of photocopied sheets of paper; some described the
experiences children would have at the nursery, including aspects of
the curriculum, food, rest, outings and so on, others tended to focus
on the 'rules' of the nursery – the hours, the fees and method of
payment, and items which should be brought to the nursery when
the child started.

Although only slightly more than half the nurseries reported
having a written admissions policy describing how places were
allocated, a somewhat larger number – approximately 80 per cent –
appeared to convey this and other relevant information (such as
payment, holidays and period of notice) in the form of a written
contract with parents. However, although three quarters of nurseries
reported having a policy on equal opportunities, only one third of
these – 25 per cent overall – routinely made this available to parents.
In the main, these policy statements had been drawn up by, and for,
the host organisation of the nursery: rarely, then, did they have the
specific interests of the nursery staff or users in mind. Likewise,
although it is now accepted good practice to monitor ethnicity, less
than half the nurseries appeared to involve parents in collecting this
information. In so doing, it seems likely that nurseries may be
missing valuable opportunities to learn from parents about differences of language, diet, culture, child rearing practices, all of which

would contribute to ensuring that nursery provision was sensitive to today's multicultural society.

When a child first starts at nursery, it can be a traumatic time for parents as well as children and questionnaire responses indicate that most nurseries are very aware of the significance of this 'settling-in' time, and had developed a range of tactics to ease the process. Some, for example, stressed the importance of having a key worker at this stage, in order that the parent, as well as the child, was able to develop an intimate relationship with at least one member of staff. It was also the custom of most nurseries to adopt a flexible approach to the build-up of the child's attendance and the parent's withdrawal, and, because of this, some nurseries waived the first few week's fees: only two nurseries appeared to adopt a more structured approach than this, one stating that the settling-in period comprised three initial visits by child and parent, the other that it comprised four. In addition several nurseries commented that at this stage they always clarified to parents that they could call into or telephone the nursery at any time.

In general, our information suggests that parents were positive about the welcome extended to them. A few, however, shared the following view:

> To start with, I didn't find the nursery friendly at all – this is a time when the nursery should be sympathetic to child and parents.

Such parents were nonetheless able to make some positive suggestions about how things could be improved and it would appear significant that the following were made with some consistency:

> Staff should be introduced personally so that you know their names.

> Staff should wear name badges.

During the settling-in period and subsequently, it is acknowledged that having a specific space or room designated for parents' use can underline the fact that parents are welcome in the nursery. It may to some extent be a reflection of the fact that many of the parent users of these nurseries were in employment or studying – and therefore had limited time to spend in the nursery – but of the 95 nurseries completing the questionnaire, only four had a room for the exclusive use of parents. Although a further 21 nurseries reported that parents could share a room where they might have a drink and perhaps the occasional chat, overall this still meant that only about a quarter of the nurseries were able to reinforce the concept of partnership with parents by offering them some form of accommodation.

Communication between parents and professionals

The development of partnership relies on communication, whereby parents have confidence in staff and staff, in turn, become acquainted with the family, its habits and customs and are thus better placed to understand the child. As Braun (1992) points out this means not only that communication needs to be frequent but that advantage must be taken of opportunities as they arise, as well as there being planned contacts.

The nursery questionnaire sought information about the methods nurseries use for matters of general communication with parents. Notice boards appeared to be the most commonly adopted approach and were referred to by 93 of the 95 nurseries. In addition, notes or letters to parents were mentioned by 86 nurseries, regular newsletters by 67, nursery-to-home notebooks by 24 and parent post boxes by 13, whilst methods such as meetings, verbal exchanges, telephone, reports, daily diary or log and suggestion box were much less frequently cited.

Whilst visiting nurseries some of these methods were examined in more detail. For example, the parents' log in one nursery was a large book kept by the door in which staff made daily notes about each child, mainly in relation to eating and sleeping patterns and their main activities on that day. In another, a daily report was written for each child – in the format 'I ate... I slept... Things I did today... General comments...' – and was pinned to a notice board for parents to read (or take with them) when they collected children.

Observations in the smaller group of nurseries also highlighted that the beginning and end of the day were the most likely times of contact between parents and staff. Some warm and friendly chats were observed on these occasions, with parents appearing quite at ease in the nursery setting and happy to stay so long as their time commitments permitted. Sometimes the staff support to parents extended beyond their common child focus, such as in a college nursery when parents were feeling exam pressure. Here the staff were prepared to listen to parents' anxieties and worries about the future and as one parent put it:

> Nursery staff encouraged me to attend college, reassured me and had a big influence on my attitude to attendance.

In another nursery when a first-time parent became worried that her baby had not settled for some days, the nursery staff concluded that he was under-nourished and hungry. Inviting the mother to come to the nursery at her earliest convenience, the nursery manager discussed the situation with great sensitivity, allowing the mother to keep control of the decision to start introducing solids into the baby's diet.

Assessing individual children's progress is clearly an important area for staff-parent communication. Analysis of the questionnaire returns suggests that over 80 per cent of the nurseries (77) involve parents in this process. However, individual responses tend to imply that rather than this being a planned and relatively structured process, in many instances, a rather more non-specific, if not ad hoc, approach is adopted. The following selected quotations give a flavour of the range of responses given in this respect:

> Parents can be present during assessments, and assessments are discussed with them.

> Involvement with reviews.

> Parents are encouraged to discuss all areas of development and to look in folders and at developmental sheets.

> By communication with parents.

> Reporting to parents.

> At parents' meetings.

> We tell parents any necessary information vital to development and learning.

> ... daily contact or conversations with staff.

On the other hand, 12 nurseries made it quite clear that they did **not** involve parents in monitoring children's development. One commented, for example:

> (It) has been done with one child but only due to parental concern.

And another:

> Objections can be raised at parents' meetings.

Only five nurseries responding to the postal questionnaire reported that parents did not have access to their child's developmental records. However, although 29 stated that all parents would have seen their child's records during the previous year, there was evidence to suggest that not all parents took advantage of this. Indeed, the extent to which nurseries actively encouraged parental involvement and participation in this respect varied widely, with three distinct approaches being identifiable. In the 'pro-active' group (comprising about 20 nurseries) records were discussed with parents at a formal review or parents' meeting, or the child's key worker discussed them informally with parents. In the 'inactive' group, comprising the majority of nurseries, a typical response was 'parents just have to ask'. Only one nursery actually **discouraged** the involvement of parents in seeing their children's records, its response being: 'We don't really advertise the fact'!

It would seem, then, that some nurseries may need to review their procedures for supporting and encouraging parents' access to records. On the other hand, in the course of our site visits we observed that some nurseries had developed quite detailed mechanisms whereby parents could became closely involved in their child's learning. 'Parent packs' provide one such example: these comprised (for each child) a folder containing a selected book, a list of suggested questions parents might ask in order to stimulate the child's concentration and language development, and a comment sheet on which parents were requested to summarise how the child had found the exercise. The book generally encouraged the use of concepts such as big/small, long/short, colours or numbers and when the folder was returned to the nursery, a staff member would go through the book again with the child, encouraging recollection and discussion of the story.

A further important aspect of staff-parent communication involves ensuring that parents have opportunities to learn about the nursery's overall philosophy and methods, why certain activities and materials are used, or certain skills encouraged. This type of discussion enables parents to gain a broader picture of the development of children's skills and learning, and to satisfy themselves that their child is supported in a rich learning environment, rather than assuming that 'he just plays all day'. The questionnaire asked how often parents' **group** meetings were held: 35 nurseries responded that such a meeting was held at least four times a year; 19 that one was held three times a year; 13 that there were two meetings annually, and five that there was one. Eleven stated that they had never held such a meeting, although two of these indicated that this situation was currently under review.

It is also recommended (see, for example, National Children's Bureau, 1991) that staff should meet with individual sets of parents between one and three times a year. Meetings such as these are intended to offer opportunities to discuss individual children's progress in some detail, as well as to enable parents to raise any matters of concern. The questionnaire returns suggest that whilst 34 nurseries did hold this type of individual meeting regularly (usually on a monthly, termly or annual basis), the remainder tended to adopt a more ad hoc approach, with many indeed expressing a preference not to have meetings but to rely on informal ongoing contact with parents. Only ten nurseries indicated that they did not hold this type of meeting at all, but relied entirely on ongoing contact with parents.

The tendency of most nurseries to rely on informal methods of communication undoubtedly reflects the difficulty many of their parent users – in employment or studying – would have in attending day time meetings. One of the ways in which some nurseries attempted to overcome this was by holding meetings in the evening and just over half the nurseries responding to the postal questionnaire reported arranging a creche when evening meetings were held. Likewise a similar proportion of nurseries cited a range of ways in which they endeavoured to overcome the potential language or literacy difficulties of parents: these included putting up notices in a range of languages, having translation and interpretation services available and generally being able to spend adequate time with parents on a one-to-one basis to ensure that the communication had been understood.

Parental involvement in the running of nurseries
Because the parent group of each nursery comprises individuals of different skills and time available to contribute to the nursery, it is important that there is a range of ways in which parents can become involved in nursery activities. The 11 most common forms of parental involvement – as cited by the nurseries – are listed in Table 8.3.

This gives the overall impression of a fairly high degree of parental involvement, with each of the 95 nurseries reporting having at least three of these forms available, and the majority no less than eight. Nonetheless, this gives no indication of the number of parents so involved. One such case in point is parental involvement by sitting on an advisory/steering group or management committee: Midland

Table 8.3   Forms of parental involvement and number of nurseries reporting their availability

Daily conversation with staff	93
Dropping in at the nursery	89
Involvement in fund-raising	88
Participation in social events	83
Formal meetings with staff by arrangement	77
Through parents' meetings	76
Serving on advisory group/steering group	62
Involvement in publicity	49
Contributing to a newsletter	45
Serving on a management committee	45
Participation in training/discussion groups	25

Bank recommends nurseries to reserve at least one place on such a body for parent representation. However, ten nurseries failed to report offering any parents such an opportunity.

Parents, nonetheless, did comment that, in their experience, nurseries did try to involve parents but that this was very difficult to achieve because of the other constraints on parents' time. Some suggested further steps that specific nurseries might take such as changing the time of meetings, having newsletters and weekend events, whilst others added:

the problem is parent apathy

and

only the parents can improve on this.

Discussion

Writing in 1989, Pugh and De'Ath concluded 'partnership is an elusive concept'. The Children Act has further emphasised the importance of partnership with parents in child care matters generally, but particularly insofar as young children are concerned. The overall picture conveyed by this research is that nurseries are increasingly aware of the importance of partnership and, in the main, are actively seeking to extend the ways in which parents may become involved. However, while a transition has now begun, much yet remains to be achieved.

As many practitioners are aware, 'partnership' is one of those concepts which sounds straightforward enough, but the achievement of which is rather more complex. Assuming the availability of resources, there are a number of positive steps which nurseries might take to facilitate partnership and parental involvement more generally. For instance, this research would suggest that if individual nurseries were to review their practice of introducing parents to the nursery, parents would be more likely to be better informed about the ethos of the nursery, be more acquainted with the roles and responsibilities of the respective members of staff and sense that their presence in the nursery was quite appropriate. Likewise, the introduction of ethnic monitoring and the positive sharing of children's developmental records are two means by which parents could significantly contribute to nursery practice – both generally and in relation to individual children. The importance of having a readily available mechanism whereby parents are able to feedback their views – positive and negative – needs also to be recognised, both by the holding of parent group meetings and by having accessible a simple, but written, complaints procedure. As chapter 4 showed, less than half the nurseries had a written procedure in this respect.

These matters do of course raise the issue of resources – those of both time and money and these need to be addressed. A further issue concerns the training of staff. Few staff working in nurseries today – at either the management or practitioner level – have had the benefit of training which focuses on building relationships with parents or other adult carers. In-service training aimed at both raising awareness and the development of skills would seem to have an important contribution to make in this respect.

Partnership is, however, a two-way process and whilst there is much that nurseries might do to facilitate it, parents, too, need to have a commitment to it. Our contact with parent users indicates that, whilst they are concerned to have confidence and trust in the nursery they use, they rarely have specific criteria or reference points which they can use to assess the quality of provision their child is receiving. Furthermore, circumstances often mean that the degree of choice which parents can exercise in relation to where a child is placed is invariably quite limited. The fact that many working and studying parents do not have a great deal of time to devote to playing a part in the nursery also needs to be recognised. In combination, then, these factors suggest that parent-users are unlikely to represent the potent force in moulding practice that is often anticipated. This being the case, it becomes all the more important that there can be confidence in the system of public monitoring and registration as operated by local authorities.

9. Quality day care for children: moving forward

Whether or not it attracts universal approval, it is an increasingly common feature of contemporary society that, from early childhood, children experience non-parental day care, quite frequently on a full-time basis. The reasons for this are many, reflecting wider social, demographic and economic trends. In consequence, child care is not the exclusive domain of parents or providers but raises issues of equality and responsibility within the family and the workplace and has implications for employers, for local communities and society at large. Although, then, this research has focused on day nurseries, it has implications not only for nursery practice but for the wider social policy context also.

This chapter is comprised of three sections. As each of the preceding chapters has concluded with a summary, the chapter begins, not by repeating all of these, but by highlighting the most important themes that emerge. The second part of the chapter poses a number of questions raised by the research and considers what steps might be taken to improve the quality of nursery practice. Finally, attention is drawn to the importance of avoiding narrow policies in relation to child care and the need for central government to adopt a more strategic role in relation to a national child care agenda.

The main messages of the research

Before discussing the main themes of the research in terms of children's experiences, parental participation and the challenges encountered by nurseries, we start with a few preliminary comments. The aim of this research was to examine nursery provision from the perspective of children's well-being. One of the standard approaches to evaluating a service – that of seeking the views of its consumers – is relevant to meeting this aim. However, in the case of very young children, there are difficulties associated not only with seeking their views, but with the meaning to be attached to any views obtained. For this reason, our research methods included extensive observation of children in the nursery setting. It is important to emphasise that these observations revealed a group of children who, for the most part, appeared quite happy and contented and that we witnessed no instances of glaringly dangerous or abusive practice. Indeed, drawing on our experience of nurseries generally, we have little doubt that what this group of nurseries is providing is a service which is generally above the average prevailing in nurseries today. However, given our current knowledge of young children's developmental needs, the question must surely be asked 'Is this good enough?'.

Children's experience

The research demonstrates that much of nursery practice in relation to individual children takes inadequate account of the state of current knowledge about young children's developmental needs. Three aspects warrant particular attention.

- **Stability, continuity and 'significant' relationships**
  Notwithstanding the importance of these factors to young children's future social, emotional and intellectual development, nurseries rarely gave them overriding priority in either the deployment of staff or the overall organisation of the nursery day. More specifically, although the majority of nurseries professed to having adopted the key worker model, our observations suggest that this system is quite frequently misunderstood and only partially implemented in practice. Moreover, important as stability, continuity and 'significant' relationships are for all young children, they are especially important to babies and toddlers. In this respect, our observations suggest that nurseries need to give much greater attention to the needs of this particular group of children.

- **Stimulating activities and experiences**
  The research evidence shows that nurseries are becoming increasingly aware of the need to provide children with a range of interesting and stimulating activities and experiences. Accordingly much consideration is given to the purchase of equipment and to arranging visits to and out of the nursery. However there was rather less evidence of an appreciation of the role of adults in encouraging and guiding children's natural

instinct to explore and discover. Indeed, in this respect, the research shows that not all nursery staff have the relevant skills and/or inclination to work with children in this manner, a situation which was not improved by the fact that few nurseries had access to support based on a professional background and training in the education of young children.

- **Taking account of individual differences, needs and wishes**
  It would be quite wrong of us to convey the impression that day nurseries never treat children as individuals but only as part of a group. Likewise it would be equally wrong to suggest that children in day nurseries are the subjects of a predetermined nursery routine, rigidly adhered to. However, our observations do suggest that substantial numbers of staff fail to recognise – and to value – the importance of differences between children. Evidence of this was particularly disturbing on two fronts. First it appeared to be the exception, rather than the rule, for individual children's progress to be actively monitored, for written records of this progress to be maintained, or for work with individual children to be planned. Furthermore, although generally nurseries appeared to be making progress in developing anti-discriminatory practice, there was nonetheless a depressing lack of awareness of the need to convey positive images of all ethnic groups and cultures to all children.

The fact that these findings emerge from research carried out in nurseries where the standards of practice in operation would generally be regarded as being of at least average quality is particularly disconcerting. Before considering this further, the research evidence in relation to parental involvement and to some of the difficulties faced by nurseries is discussed.

Parental involvement
While the research suggests that nurseries appear to welcome the notion of partnership with parents and that parents feel they ought to be more involved in nursery affairs generally, it has also revealed that parental involvement in the nurseries was not particularly high. The data suggest that a number of factors contribute to this:

- **Time constraints**
  Although one might be tempted to dismiss parents' comments about lack of time as mere excuses, the very real time constraints on parents have to be acknowledged. With work or study

commitments, it is not necessarily straightforward to attend day time meetings and, in any event, these may pose difficulties for the staff. Likewise, family and domestic commitments limit the availability of both parents and staff for evening meetings.

- **Choice**
  The fact that their access to nursery provision was facilitated, and often subsidised, means that many of the parent users involved in this research might be considered to be 'advantaged' parents, most parents not having the same degree of access to child care. On the other hand, since their access was confined to a specific facility, the degree of choice which they were able to exercise was somewhat circumscribed. This would certainly appear to have implications for the extent to which parents might wish to be seen as complaining, and likewise to have the effect of restricting parents' ability to 'vote with their feet'.

- **Expectations**
  Parents do not necessarily have very high or clear expectations of the provision nurseries should be making. Indeed, as became apparent from our interviews with parents, deciding to place their child in the nursery was only one part of a much larger decision concerning return to employment or study. Furthermore for many, the fact that the nursery was 'approved' by an employer or registered with the local authority represented an acceptable yardstick by which to assess the quality offered. However, much as local authority registration and the new standards of the 1989 Children Act are to be welcomed, few parents appear to be aware of what these standards are, and that they are intended to represent no more than **minimum** standards.

The barriers, then, to parents becoming more actively involved in moulding day nursery practice and policy, and to making partnership with parents more of a reality are not inconsiderable.

Nurseries and the challenges posed in providing day care

The research has highlighted the tremendous variety which currently exists in the size and patterns of management and ownership of nurseries. However, despite these differences, there is a commonality about the challenges and difficulties which nurseries face. A number of these are singled out for attention here.

- **Achieving a balance between affordability and quality**
  This is perhaps the most fundamental challenge faced by all

nurseries. Child care is labour intensive and therefore does not come cheaply. **Quality** child care is even more expensive. Furthermore although parents may receive a subsidy to meet the fees, few nurseries are subsidised and are required to meet the full costs of running the service through the fees they charge. Thus whilst marketplace principles dictate that the level of fees must not exceed that which will ensure a full take up of the available places, expenditure cannot exceed guaranteed income, and desirable improvements with cost implications have to wait. A number of examples of this have been highlighted in the preceding chapters.

- **Valuing and developing child care skills**
  The research confirms – what others have already pointed out – that working with young children is an under-valued occupation in our society. Thus, despite the demanding nature of the work and the fact that in these nurseries a higher than average percentage of staff were professionally qualified, working conditions were not good and levels of remuneration were low. Combined, these factors do not contrive to make child care an attractive profession, with consequent difficulties in recruiting and retaining staff.

- **Management issues**
  Our observations lead us to conclude that one of the casualties of the current system of financing nurseries is that insufficient attention is paid to the management needs of running a nursery. The day-to-day demands of running a nursery should not be underestimated, and require a high degree of flexibility and adaptability on the part of the nursery manager. However many nursery managers seem to be drawn (sometimes quite willingly) into substantial, 'hands-on' working with children, leaving them limited time for more strategic matters, the general running of the nursery, the supervision of staff and developing practice. Furthermore, the role of management committees is not always entirely clear, leaving considerable scope for ambiguity and confusion concerning the respective responsibilities of management committees and nursery managers.

- **Practice issues**
  The above management issues clearly have a knock-on effect on practice. Combined with factors such as the lack of adult space and staff supervision, the length of the nursery day and, in particular, the lack of non-contact time, these contribute to it being

relatively rare for nurseries to engage in detailed advanced planning of the curriculum or in monitoring individual children's progress.

- **The relative isolation of nurseries**
  The research also highlights that nurseries can be quite isolated professionally: management committees are understandably more business driven than child-oriented; there are limited opportunities for in-house professional supervision and development, and most nurseries appear to be, at best, on the periphery of any local-authority-initiated child care training and development network.

Improving the quality of nursery practice: some suggestions

Notwithstanding the wider issues of availability and affordability, there are a number of relatively low cost measures which could be taken to improve the quality of day nursery provision. Employers – protecting their investment in child care – and local authorities – with their registration, inspection and reviewing functions – are well placed to work alongside individual nurseries in this respect. The following are some broad suggestions which seem to merit further consideration:

- It should be an accepted part of the annual inspection process that nurseries produce a development plan for the next year, this being a collaborative exercise between nursery staff and management committees or owners. In turn, local authorities (and possibly employers using the nursery) would consider how they could facilitate the achievement of plans. One aspect highlighted by this approach would be the training needs of staff, managers and management committee representatives.
- Notwithstanding the above, local authorities, possibly in collaboration with adult education centres, should ensure that all day nurseries have access to resource material concerning young children.
- As part of their inspection, local authorities should ensure that there is a core group of staff designated to work with babies and toddlers, and that all such staff have undertaken some training in relation to working with very young children – and facilitate this.

- If the existing staff group does not include at least one staff member with a professional background in early years education, access to such a person should be negotiated at least on a sessional basis.
- All staff should have 'protected' non-contact time in order that they can **plan** the curriculum. This is especially important in nurseries where a high proportion of the children attend on a full-time basis.
- In order to promote parental involvement and to ensure that parents are generally more effective users, local authorities should consider producing a concise and impartial, user-friendly parents' guide aimed at describing the authority's registration standards and providing guidance to help parents assess the quality of individual facilities.

Steps such as these would undoubtedly have an impact on the quality of nursery provision. As all providers will be aware, however, although these partially address the resource issue, many of the difficulties associated with achieving a balance between affordability and quality remain. Indeed, even if fully implemented, these steps alone would not address the fundamental limitations inherent in our current child care system: availability and affordability; staff training; salary levels.

Moving the child care issue forward

Earlier in this chapter, we raised the question 'Is this good enough?' Given our knowledge of the developmental needs of young children and of current provision, the answer to this question must surely be that improvements are required and that our approach needs to be based on a belief in the importance of investing in children as the citizens of the future. Equally, if children's well-being is to be taken into account, the issue of child care cannot be divorced from the wider question of the relationship between paid work and family responsibilities more generally. In this respect, it is clear that a lead is required from central government.

The need for a more wide-ranging approach is clearly evident at the current time of writing. Thus, following the independent reports of the National Commission for Education (1993) and the Royal Society of Arts (Ball, 1994), senior politicians of all parties have declared their commitment to the wider availability of publicly-provided pre-school education. Should such a commitment turn into reality it is to be welcomed. However, what such proposals do not address are the needs of **working** parents or their children: at best nursery education would not be available before children reached the age of three years, and then only on a part-time basis. As such, then, these proposals do little to address the wider issue of combining work and family responsibilities – a necessary reality for many parents – and of family-friendly employment policies and practices more generally.

In concluding this research, we would urge central government to take a lead in establishing a national child care agenda. Given the current need to respond to the Council of European Communities Recommendation on Child Care (92/241), the time for this is opportune. Key components of such an agenda need to be:

- the setting up of a government working group comprising all the significant central government departments, as well as employers and relevant early childhood organisations;
- a review of family, equality and labour market policies with a brief to make recommendations regarding their development and coordination;
- a commitment to ensuring that existing services cater for children's need for education as well as their need for care and to the development of further services on this basis;
- a review of the training requirements and salaries of those working with young children;
- the development of a mechanism whereby partnership between local authorities, employers and providers can be encouraged at the local level and consideration given to meeting the community's need for quality child care which is at the same time both affordable and accessible;
- a strategy for monitoring progress on this agenda.

It will clearly take some time for such an agenda to be worked through. However, it is in all our interests – those of children, their parents and society as a whole – that such an agenda be set up and that it is accorded a high priority. We owe that to our children, their families and the future.

Bibliography

Association of Metropolitan Authorities (1991) *Children First: Services for Young Children.* AMA

Bain, A and Barnett, L (1980) *The Design of a Day Care System in a Nursery Setting for Children Under Five,* Final Report to DHSS of an action research project 1975-79. Tavistock Institute of Human Relations

Balaguer, I, Mestres, J and Penn, H (1991) *Quality in Services for Young Children: A Discussion Paper.* European Commission Childcare Network

Ball, C (1994) *Start Right: The Importance of Early Learning.* Royal Society for the Encouragement of the Arts, Manufacturers and Commerce

Barnardo's (1992) *Support the Parents, Support the Children.* A video produced by Barnardo's. (Now withdrawn). See the Training Notes to accompany the film

Berrueta-Clement, J, Scweinhart, L, Barnett, W, Epstein, A and Weikart, D (1984) *Changed Lives: The Effects of the Perry Preschool Program on Youths Through Age 19.* High/Scope Research Institute

Bowlby, J (1952) *Maternal Care and Mental Health.* WHO, Geneva

Braun, D (1992) 'Working with Parents', *in* Pugh, G (ed) *Contemporary Issues in the Early Years.* Paul Chapman Publishing Ltd in association with the National Children's Bureau

Breeze, E and others (1991) *General Household Survey 1989.* HMSO

Business in the Community/Institute of Personnel Management (1993) *Corporate Culture and Caring: The Business Case for Family Friendly Provision.* Business in the Community and IPM

Choosing Child Care (1991) Voluntary Organisations Liaison Council for Under Fives, Scottish Child and Family Alliance, National Consumer Council. (A leaflet published by these organisations)

Clark, M, Robson, B and Browning M (1982) *Preschool Education and Children with Special Needs.* Report of research funded by DES 1979-81, Educational Review, University of Birmingham

Clark, M and Cheyne W (eds) (1979) *Studies in Preschool Education.* Hodder and Stoughton

Clarke-Stewart, A (1982) *Day Care.* Fontana

Clarke-Stewart, A (1991) 'Day Care in the USA' in Moss, P and Melhuish, E *Current Issues in Day Care for Young Children.* HMSO

Cohen, B (1988) *Caring for Children: Services and Policies for Childcare and Equal Opportunities in the United Kingdom.* Report for the European Commission's Childcare Network. Family Policy Studies Centre

Department of Education and Science (1990) *Starting with Quality: Report of the Committee of Inquiry into the Educational Experiences Offered to Three and Four-Year-Olds.* Rumbold Report. HMSO

Department of Health (1991) *The Children Act 1989 Guidance and Regulations Volume 2: Family Support, Day Care and Educational Provision for Young Children.* HMSO

Department of Health (1992) *Choosing with Care: The Report of the Committee of Inquiry into the Selection, Development and Management of Staff in Children's Homes.* HMSO

Drummond, M J, Rouse, D and Pugh, G (1992) *Making Assessment Work: Values and principles in assessing young children's learning.* NES Arnold/National Children's Bureau

Education Select Committee (House of Commons) (1989) *Educational Provision for the Under Fives*, Vol II. HMSO

Elfer, P and Wedge, D (1992) 'Defining, measuring and supporting quality', *in* Pugh, G (ed.) *Contemporary Issues in the Early Years.* Paul Chapman Publishing in association with the National Children's Bureau

Equal Opportunities Commission (1990) *The Key to Real Choice: An Action Plan for Childcare.* EOC

Ferri, E, Birchall, D, Gingell, V and Gipps, C (1981) *Combined Nursery Centres: a New Approach to Education and Day Care.* Macmillan

Finch, S (1993) *Consultancy Report on Network Nurseries.* Unpublished report for University of Luton, Department of External Affairs

Garland, C and White, S (1980) *Children and Day Nurseries: Management and Practice in Nine London Day Nurseries.* Grant McIntyre

Goldschmied, E (1989) *Infants at Work.* A video available from the National Children's Bureau

Goldschmied, E and Hughes, A (1992) *Heuristic Play with Objects.* A video available from the National Children's Bureau

Goldschmied, E and Jackson, S (1994) *People Under Three.* Routledge

Harms, T and Clifford, R (1980) *Early Childhood Environment Rating Scale.* Teacher's College Press, Columbia University, New York

Hennessy, E, Martin, S, Moss, P and Melhuish, E (1992) *Children and Day Care: Lessons from research.* Paul Chapman

Hogg, C and Harker, L (1992) *The Family Friendly Employer: Examples from Europe.* The Day Care Trust

Holtermann, S (1992) *Investing in Young Children: costing an education and day care service.* National Children's Bureau

Kids' Clubs Network (1991) *Guidelines of Good Practice for Out of School Care Schemes.* Kids' Clubs Network

Lazar, T, Darlington, R, Murray, H and Snipper, A (1982) 'Lasting Effects of Early Education', *Monograph of Society for Research in Child Development*, Vol 47, no 2-3

Lindon, J and Lindon, L (1993) *Caring for the Under 8s: Working to achieve good practice.* Macmillan

Lindon, J (1993) *Child Development from Birth to Eight: A Practical Focus.* National Children's Bureau

Marsh, A and McKay, S (1993) 'Families, work and the use of childcare', *Employment Gazette*, August

Marshall, T (1982) 'Infant care: a day nursery under the microscope', *Social Work Service*, Vol 32, no 2-3

McCail, G (1991) *Pre-Five Environment Quality Rating Scale*. Moray House College of Education, Edinburgh

Melhuish, E (1991) 'Research Issues in Day Care', *in* Moss, P and Melhuish, E (eds) *Current Issues in Day Care for Young Children*. HMSO

Ministry of Health (1968) Circular 37/68.

Moss, P (1992) 'Perspectives from Europe' *in* Pugh, G (ed.) *Contemporary Issues in the Early Years*. Paul Chapman Publishing in association with The National Children's Bureau

Moss, P and Melhuish, E (1991) 'Future Directions for Day Care Policy and Research' *in* Moss, P and Melhuish, E (eds) *Current Issues in Day Care for Young Children*. HMSO

Moss, P and Melhuish, E (eds) (1991) *Current Issues in Day Care for Young Children*. HMSO

National Childminding Association (1991) *Setting the Standards: Guidelines on Good Practice in Registering Childminders*. National Childminding Association

National Children's Bureau Under Fives Unit (1990) *A Policy for Young Children: A Framework for Action*. National Children's Bureau

National Children's Bureau (1991) *Young Children in Group Day Care: Guidelines for Good Practice*. National Children's Bureau

National Commission on Education (1993) *Learning to Succeed*. Heinemann

National Consumer Council (1991) *Daycare Services for Under-Fives: A Consumer View*. June

Open University (1991) *Working with Under Fives: An In-service Training Pack*. Open University

Parry, M and Archer, H (1974) *Pre-school Education*. Schools Council Research Studies, Macmillan Education

Penn, H (1991) *Partnership in the Early Years: An examination of local authority initiatives in developing partnership projects with the private sector in developing nursery provision*. Unpublished INLOGOV seminar paper

Penn, H and Riley, K (1992) *Managing Services for the Under Fives*. Longman

Pre-school Playgroups Association (1993) *Aiming for Quality*. (Accreditation Scheme)

Pugh, G (1988) *Services for Under Fives: Developing a co-ordinated approach*. National Children's Bureau

Pugh, G (ed.) (1992) *Contemporary Issues in the Early Years*. Paul Chapman Publishing

Pugh, G and De'Ath, E (1989) *Working Towards Partnership in the Early Years*, National Children's Bureau

Statham, J and Brophy, J (1992) Using the 'Early Childhood Environment Rating Scale in playgroups', *Educational Research*, Volume 34, No2

Sylva, K (1994) 'The Impact of Early Learning on Children's Later Development', *in* Ball, C (ed.) *Start Right: The Importance of Early Learning*. Royal Society for the Encouragement of the Arts, Manufactures and Commerce

Sylva, K and David, T (1990) 'Quality education in preschool provision', *Local Government Policy Making*, Vol 17, No3

Sylva, K, Roy, C and Painter, M (1980) *Childwatching at Playgroup and Nursery School*. Grant McIntyre

Van der Eyken, W (1984) *Day Nurseries in Action: a national study of local authority day nurseries in England, 1975-83.* Final Report to the DHSS, University of Bristol, Department of Child Health

Whitebook, M, Howes, C and Phillips, D (1989) *The National Childcare Staffing Study.* Childcare Employee Project, Oakland, USA

Williams, P (Forthcoming) *Making Sense of Quality: a review of approaches to quality in early childhood services.* Early Childhood Unit, National Children's Bureau

Appendix 1: Modified rating scale used in the project (adapted from McCail, 1991)

1. Policy and Management, including Evaluation, Assessment and Record Keeping

	INADEQUATE 1	2	MINIMAL 3	4	GOOD 5	6	EXCELLENT 7
I Aims and Plans and Evaluation	No evaluation of the facility takes place and there are no long-term plans for the facility.		Sporadic evaluation of the facility arising, usually, from some complaint. The staff take the lead but may involve a few parents. Plans for improvements may then be drawn up. Daily programme evaluations done briefly or haphazardly.		Annual open evaluation of the facility by the management group, involving the setting of objectives for the forthcoming year. Broad aims are set, eg to provide a caring service, a service accountable to its managers and users which has due regard to safety aspects, an education service. Regular daily room evaluation is linked to forward planning.		As 5, but the annual evaluation is undertaken by the total group management, staff and parents. Broad aims are set as in 5 and the means by which they are to be achieved are also specified. This evaluation, written out, is publicised and available to all concerned with the facility.
II Management Structures and Responsibilities	Staff roles are not clarified.		A chain of command, but how this operates is not always clear to parents or to outside professionals.		How management structures operate is open and clear to all, including parents. Management and senior staff responsive to the conditions of work of staff members and the needs of parents. Correct legal procedures always adhered to.		As 5, but unless the facility is directly parent-managed, an advisory group exists on which parents are strongly represented. Open discussion takes place, with the whole group involved, about any major initiatives or changes.

Chain of command involves senior management taking responsibility in all areas of the facility's operation.

III Admission Policy	No particular policy on admissions.	Policy on admissions is known to staff and parents but is not written down.	Clear written policy on admissions which involves equal opportunities. Clear enrolment priorities based on consultation with relevant agencies (eg health visitors) to encourage children with special needs or from racial minorities to apply.	As 5, and policy discussed and agreed by all parents and staff. Voluntary ethnic monitoring of families.
IV Boundaries for Children	Discipline is ad hoc, and although it does not usually involve negative action it is not consistent. Staff reactions to children's wrong-doing depend more upon the consequences of the action than the nature of the deed.	Unacceptable behaviour is quickly identified and dealt with but staff do not always explain the reasons for their actions to children involved or their parents.	Staff are consistent in the limits they set for children, informing and consulting their parents where possible. Acceptable social behaviour encouraged by staff modelling considerate attitudes; unacceptable behaviour is quickly identified and dealt with and the reasons are explained to the children involved, and to their parents also if the problem is persistent.	As 5. In addition, staff adopt a democratic and open style which involves parents and facilitates discussion between adult-child and among the children themselves.
V Children's Records	No systematic records kept, though information may sometimes be	Records are kept on each child who is a consistent user comprising emergency, health and family information. There	Records are kept for each child who is a consistent user comprising emergency, health and family information. Such	As 5. Also, parents are regularly consulted about their children's records and regularly contribute to them.

	recorded eg for a child with special needs.	is not, however, a facility policy on confidentiality.	records are open to the parents concerned and to professionals involved with the child but otherwise closed. Profiles are also kept (regularly updated by observation in the facility), which record the child's progress on a broad front – interpersonal, physical, linguistic, cognitive. These are passed on with the child to infant school.	A network of appropriate contacts has been built up from whom relevant information is regularly received (eg health visitor, GP, social worker).	
VI Personnel	Staff are not aware of their own or the facility's rights and obligations.	The rights and obligations of the employees and of the facility are known and adhered to. The selection of volunteers is, however, ad hoc. All staff have both job descriptions and contracts of service.	The management committee has adopted the legal requirements on employees' rights/obligations and a policy which sets out clearly what is expected before the volunteers take up their duties.	The management committee, parents and staff have together negotiated or accepted (as appropriate) a policy on employees and volunteers which clearly sets out employees'/facility's rights and obligations. It also regulates the recruitment, selection, responsibilities, accountability and training of volunteers.	
VII Style of Management	Nursery Manager has total control over what happens in the nursery and takes all decisions on her/his own.	Some other staff involved in some decision-making about nursery practice.	Decisions about changes in practice routinely referred to staff groups, and their opinions taken into account.	Decisions are taken after full consultation with staff and parents and/or management committee.	
VIII Complaints Procedure	No complaints procedure.	Parents can make complaints only to the nursery manager.	Written and publicised complaints procedure.		

In all categories, 7 is not given unless parents are ACTIVELY INVOLVED
IV and V: for a 5. parents should be informed.

2. Adult Cooperation and Development

	INADEQUATE 1	2	MINIMAL 3	4	GOOD 5	6	EXCELLENT 7
I Staff Qualifications and Experience	Little or no relevant experience and few qualifications among the staff.		Staff have qualifications in most of the relevant (see 5) areas and experience in all of them, though they may be, in some cases, somewhat out of date.		Staff qualifications and experience cover (between them): children's development and play; practical aspects of children's play; working with adults, including parents; children's health, safety and nutrition; aspects of child protection. The head of the facility possesses a good working knowledge of all these areas and specialised knowledge in at least one area.		As 5. In addition staff have taken advantage of in-service training opportunities to deepen and/or bring up to date own areas of expertise and to widen knowledge and acquire new skills in another relevant area. When there is a minimum of 3 staff members including domestic staff, the staff are multiracial/ethnic and of both sexes.
II Opportunities for Professional Growth	Infrequent staff meetings. No in-service training. No professional library facility.		Staff meetings limited to administrative concerns. No in-service training plan for staff. Limited professional library (eg few books, magazines or curriculum materials to improve staff performance).		Regular staff meetings to review progress and plan ahead; these include staff development and team building activities, and individual consultation/advice or supervision/appraisal. Plans for orienting new staff members. Good professional library, current material on wide variety of subjects readily available.		Everything in 5. In addition in-service training includes workshops and courses available in community as well as training in staff meetings, which is selectively open to parents. Support available for in-service training (eg released time, travel costs, etc.), with priority for staff acquisitions of skills/knowledge needed by facility. Planned sharing of professional materials among staff and parents. Training available for committee or Board members as appropriate.

	1	3	5	7
III Provision for Parents	No provision for parent-parent or parent-staff information exchange, or parent involvement in playroom. Parents discouraged from observing or being included in programme.	Parents given minimal information and limited possibilities for involvement (eg information only concerning rules, fees, attendance schedule; minimal contact at children's arrival and departure. Little attempt to make parents welcome.	Parent/staff information exchanged at regular intervals (eg through pre-entry home visits, parent consultations, in newsletter, etc) parents made aware of approach practised at facility (eg through information sheets, videos, parents' meetings). Parents welcomed into play room (eg to eat lunch with child, bath own new baby).	Everything in 5 plus provision of information on parenting, health care etc. together with support for less confident parents. Parents' input regularly sought in planning and evaluating programme. Parents involved in decision-making roles along with staff (eg parent representatives on board).
IV Wider Team Consultation	No contact with any care or health professional	Some care or health professionals (eg health visitor) visit the facility but since visits are sporadic, no regular contacts built up.	Wide consultation with parents, and relevant workers – social workers, educational consultants, relevant voluntary organisations (eg for single parent families), health visitors, GPs, community education workers and, as appropriate, with paediatricians, speech and physio-therapists, etc, all of whom offer advice to the facility about the children for whom they share a remit.	As 5. In addition, these professionals have regular meetings with parents in the facility for case conferences, observe in facility and pass on to staff and parents therapeutic exercises or regimes to be carried out with particular children. Regular or frequent contact with other pre-five provision playgroups, nursery school, other day nurseries etc.
V Adult Personal Space and Meeting Areas	No special adult areas (eg staff room, parents' room, consultation room), no suitable area for adult group	Separate adults' room (parents and staff must share) but this must be used for other activities which interfere (eg area noisy, interruptions frequent because of dual use as	Room for individual consultations, also staff room and parents' room. These may also be used for group meetings but dual use does not make time-tabling difficult.	Everything in 5 but dual use of any of these rooms is not required. SSecure adult storage of personal possessions in the playroom.

	1	2	3	4	5	6	7
	meetings during the day or individual consultations. No storage for adults' personal belongings.		office, play room, etc.). No separate facilities for consultation.		Children may sometimes 'overflow' into one or two of these rooms.		Staff allowed at least one hour per day non-contact time to plan, write-up, think etc.
VI Non-contact time	Staff not expected to plan activities ahead, or write up records.		Staff find time in 'quiet times' to do their planning and writing up.		Staff allowed at least one hour a week non-contact time to plan, record etc.		Staff allowed at least one hour per day non-contact time to plan, write-up, think etc.

I For a 7, recent in-service for most of the staff is a sine qua non; while it counts towards a high grade, if one area of expertise is altogether missing, a 5 cannot be given.

II All five items present for a 5. Parents also for a 7.

III For a 7 parents must be active; for a 5, merely informed about facility.

IV For a 5, wide contacts are regular, for a 7, professionals interact with individual children and families in the facility

3. Language and Reasoning Experiences

	INADEQUATE 1	2	MINIMAL 3	4	GOOD 5	6	EXCELLENT 7
I Understanding of Language (receptive language)	Few materials present and little use of materials to help children understand language (eg no scheduled story time daily).		Some materials, but either not available on regular basis (closed cupboards) or not regularly used for language development.		Many materials present for free choice and supervised use. At least one planned activity daily (eg reading books to children, story telling, flannel board stories, finger plays, etc.). In addition, an easy relaxed atmosphere in which talk flows and where everyone, children and adults, listens to the other and responds.		Everything in 5, plus adults provide good language model throughout day (eg give clear directions, use words exactly in descriptions). Additional activities planned for children with special needs.
	Materials: Books, records, picture Lotto and other picture card games, flannel board materials etc.						

II Using Language (expressive language)	No scheduled activities for using language (eg no children's planning time, talking about drawings, time for talking about home doings).	Some activities for using language (eg time for talking about home doings), but child language not encouraged throughout the day.	Many activities for using language available during free play, but not planned specifically for expressive language development. Adults sensitive to individuals and are ready to give time for response, or to introduce alternative strategies for children who are not yet ready to respond.	Daily plans provide a wide variety of activities for using language during free play. Opportunities to develop skills in expressing thoughts are part of a language development plan based on individual needs. Adults encourage expressive language throughout the day, often on a one-to-one basis.

Activities: puppets, finger plays, singing rhymes, answering questions, talking about experiences, interpreting pictures, dramatic play.

III Using Learning Concepts (reasoning)	Adults do not encourage the children to reason and there are no activities, materials or games to extend reasoning.	Though there are some activities, materials and games to extend reasoning, they are not readily available and the adults do not usually encourage the children to reason.	Sufficient activities, materials and games available on a regular basis. Children choose, with adults and children holding frequent discussions where reasons are sought on both sides.	Everything in 5, plus a plan for introducing concepts as children are ready, either individually or in groups. Adult/child discussions, often one-to-one, use actual events and experiences as basis for concept development (eg children learn sequence by talking about their experiences in their daily routine, or by recalling the sequence of a cooking project).

Materials: shape sorting boxes, beads. Sets of (eg) home corner crockery/cutlery. Pre-school sequence cards, same/different games, size and shape toys, sorting games.

IV **Informal use of Language**	Language outside group times primarily used by adults to control children's behaviour and to manage routines	Adults sometimes converse with children but children are asked primarily "yes/no" or short answer questions. Children's talk not encouraged.	Open-ended adult-child conversations are frequent. Language is primarily used by adults to exchange information with children and for purposeful discussion. Children's home language, accents, dialects are valued and respected. Opportunities to communicate in home language.	Adults listen to children and much open-ended conversation takes place involving every child in the room, in varying numbers and combinations. Many, however, are dialogues, adult-child and child-child. Easy, relaxed atmosphere. Staff understand how children's language develops. Adults verbally expand on ideas presented by children (eg add information, ask questions to encourage the child to talk more).
IVa **Informal Use of Language (Infants/Toddlers)**	Little or no talking to infants and toddlers.	Language used primarily to control child's behaviour (eg you mustn't do that, no).	Caregiver responds to sounds infants make, engages in verbal play with gestures, body language (eg sings to child, recites rhymes, jingles, imitates child's sounds), encourages infant by action, movement. Staff repeat what toddlers say, expanding and elaborating as appropriate.	Everything in 5, plus staff talk to child during routines, describing activity child is engaged in; encourage toddler to use words; maintain eye contact when talking to child. Adults have time to respond to toddlers' repetitive questions.

II Activities to be age-appropriate: viz., a brick hidden under blanket for infants.

4. Investigation

	INADEQUATE 1	2	MINIMAL 3	4	GOOD 5	6	EXCELLENT 7
I Programme	Little awareness of children's need to explore.		Awareness among the adults of children's exploration needs but while these are dealt with as they arise and discovery opportunities are sometimes created, there is no systematic programme.		A well-planned programme underpins a range of appropriate experiences which extend the children's curiosity about the world and their exploration of it.		As 5, but the programme is individualised and flexible, so that each child can choose his or her own route and pace, which is facilitated by the adults. Within this individualised programme, children's cooperation with each other is encouraged.
II Staff Roles	Adults have little interaction with the children in their care to further the children's exploration.		Adults seek to provide, ad hoc, for the children's need to explore the world around them.		Adults plan the programme with the needs of individual children in mind, talk to the children about the children's discoveries and encourage child–child discussion and role play.		As 5. Also adults work with individual children in whatever way is judged to be most appropriate, guiding them, supplying information, questioning them, directing them to picture books or other sources of information, facilitating their dramatic or role play or joining in with their explorations.
III Investigation Displays and Areas	Very little, if any, investigatory activity takes place within the facility. There are very few, and stereotyped, displays.		Children bring in interesting objects from time to time (eg shells) and these are displayed.		An "interest" table where displays of various objects are mounted (eg footwear, clocks and time-pieces) which children use. Children bring in objects, to start or add to a display. There is an area where toddlers are encouraged in tactile exploration.		An investigation area integrated into on-going work and current topics of interest where children on their own or in partnership with an adult explore a series of natural or man-made phenomena supplied by staff or the children. Objects exchanged

				as soon as interest in them is satisfied and further interest met in its turn (eg interest in paper, including blotting paper, leads to an interest in what soaks up water and thence to sponges). Toddlers' area as 5.
IV Natural World	An exploration which the children do is unplanned, fortuitous and not facilitated by the adults.	Children explore in facility's outdoor space and are taken on visits to park, woods or sea but in a programme which is determined by adult constraints.	Children encouraged to explore the natural world by play in the garden earth (growing things, mini-beasts) and by visits to eg the woods, sea shore. In addition, a 'natural' area in the play-room where children can investigate eg seashells, a section of tree trunk.	Curriculum aims to offer opportunities to each child to discover a range of aspects of the natural world eg focus on hot/cold, experiences with natural materials (eg sand, water).
V Community	Children are not given opportunities to extend their awareness of the community in which they live.	Facility does not extend children's discovery in the community, although there are occasional visits to eg the fire station, a farm.	Children's home experience is extended by parents working alongside the staff, by inviting community representatives (the postman, firemen, local shop keeper) into the facility and by walks around locality, trips to post letters, visits to, eg the local shops.	Children are given many opportunities to become aware of their community and of their place in it in all the ways outlined in 5, with the addition that all the adults involved, staff, parents, community representatives, know of these central aims.

5. Creative Activities

	INADEQUATE 1	2	MINIMAL 3	4	GOOD 5	6	EXCELLENT 7
I Art	Few art materials available. Regimented use of materials (mostly adult directed projects). Art materials not freely available for children to use as a free choice activity.		Some materials, for example felt-tip drawing and painting, available for free choice, but adult directed projects when all copy an adult example, predominate.		Individual expression and free choice encouraged with art materials. Variety of materials available for free choice including 3 dimensional materials (eg scrap materials).		As 5. Attempts to relate art activities to other experiences. On occasion, a child encouraged to communicate, eg. her delight in a special experience, to other children through art work (eg painting of a first railway journey; scrap model of city tower blocks). Adults responsive and encouraging. Resources ample.
II Music/ Movement	No specific provision made for music/movement activities.		Occasional provision for music/movement experiences (eg records/tapes or musical instruments or singing time).		Music provided as a free choice activity. Also adult initiated on request. Time for singing, musical instruments or movement provided several times weekly.		Space and time planned for music and movement. Variety of records or tapes, commercial and home-made instruments and dance props, freely available as age-appropriate and also as planned time with adult. As with art, attempts to relate musical activities to other experiences and activities.
III Sand/Water	No provision for sand or water play.		Some provision for sand or water play outdoors or in.		Daily provision for sand and water play outdoors or indoors, play equipment available as children's interests require eg cups, spoons, funnels, shovels, pots and pans, trucks.		Provision for sand, dry and damp, and water play outdoors and indoors with appropriate play equipment, supervision, freely available. Staff support reinforces play in relevant directions, social play,

exploratory play eg by offering changes in play equipment.

IV Dramatic and Role Play	No special provision made for dressing up or dramatic play.	Dramatic play props focused on domestic roles. Little or no provision for dramatic play involving adventure, work, transport.	Variety of age-appropriate dramatic play props including domestic, adventure, work, transport and fantasy. Space provided both indoors and outside for more active play.	Everything in 5 plus stories, pictures, trips used to enrich dramatic play.
V Bricks and Construction Kits	Few bricks and accessories or construction equipment, nor enough space to play with them.	No special brick or construction toy area, but space and bricks or construction sets available. Enough equipment for at least 2 children to play at the same time.	Special brick area set aside out of traffic, with convenient storage space, bricks and accessories for 3 or more children at a time, or special construction set area similarly equipped.	Special large area for brick play with suitable surface (eg flat rug). Variety of large and small bricks and accessories with storage to encourage independent use (eg pictures on shelves to show where bricks belong). Extra props provided to extend children's interest in, eg fire engine theme. As well as this, special construction set area with similar facilities.
VI Plastic Materials (clay, playdough, mud, snow (in season) plasticene, 'gluck')	Plasticene occasionally provided.	Modelling materials regularly provided but this is usually in the form of playdough or plasticene. Quantities may be inadequate for the permitted number of children and colours of plasticene may be mixed up.	An area provided for play with plastic materials near running water so that mess is not a problem (waterproof aprons provided for children). Plastic material provided regularly in large enough quantities for at least 3 children to experience fully its tactile qualities. Clay available at least once a week.	As 5. Children sometimes help to make up dough. Children given opportunities to experience clay with different degrees of moisture and dryness. Children encouraged to identify own modelling problems and to find own solutions. Mud is occasionally available, and snow in season.

	1	3	5	7
				Extra props provided to extend children's interest, eg bun-tins with dough.
VII Woodwork	Woodwork not provided.	Wood off-cuts, toy hammers and saws sometimes provided when adults can supervise closely.	Woodwork bench provided with a variety of wood off-cuts; small adult hammers, saws, screwdrivers, and pincers provided. Discrete adult supervision without interference except to make facilitating suggestions. A safety programme in operation.	As 5. Variety of shapes, sizes and textures of wood provided with range of small adult tools, in the use of which children initially instructed. Attempts made to relate children's woodwork to their other experiences, eg children encouraged to paint models.
VIII Programme	Little planning for interesting activities either indoors or outdoors.	Programme is either too rigid leaving no time for individual interests or too flexible (chaotic) with activities disrupting routines.	Daily programme provides balance between adult-led group activities and individual free choice, indoor and outdoor play, in addition to routine care. For extended day, part of day spent somewhere other than in playroom, preferably in fresh air.	Balance of structure and flexibility, adult-led group activities and individual free choice. Plans included to meet individual needs.

II For a rating of 7, all four must be present.
IV for 5, there must be clear options for play other than housekeeping. (Other props used infrequently may not be stored in room).
V For 5 or 7, brick area must be available for substantial portions of day. Difference between 5 and 7 is in the variety of bricks and accessories, storage organised for ease of independent use and suitable ground surface for building.
VI For 7, if clay is presented with different degrees of moisture and dryness, mud may be dispensed with.

6. Fine and Gross Motor Activities

	INADEQUATE 1	2	MINIMAL 3	4	GOOD 5	6	EXCELLENT 7
I Perceptual/Fine Motor	No developmentally appropriate fine motor play materials available for daily use.		Some developmentally appropriate play equipment. Perceptual/fine motor materials available for daily use.		Variety of developmentally appropriate perceptual/fine motor play materials in good repair, used daily by children (eg small world, screws and screwdrivers).		Everything in 5, plus materials provided in response to children's interest. Materials organised to encourage self-help; activities planned to enhance fine motor skills.
II Adult Attention (fine motor activities)	No adult attention provided when children play with perceptual/fine motor play materials.		Adult attention only to protect health and safety and to resolve conflicts.		Child given help and encouragement when needed (eg to finish jigsaw puzzle; to fit pegs into holes; shown how to use scissors, etc). Adult shows appreciation of children's work.		Everything in 5, plus adult guides children to materials on appropriate level for success. Adult plans learning sequences to develop fine motor skills (eg provides child with sewing on binka with bodkins before canvas with tapestry needles, stringing of large beads before small beads).
III Space for Gross Motor Activities	No outdoor or indoor space specifically set aside for gross motor/physical play.		Some space specifically set aside for gross motor/physical play.		Adequate space outdoors and some space indoors with planned safety precautions (eg cushioning ground cover under climbing equipment, fenced-in area).		Planned, adequate, safe, varied and pleasant space both outdoors and indoors (eg appropriate ground covers: sand, wood chips). Indoor space used in bad weather, but importance of fresh air, outdoor play, emphasised.
IV Gross Motor Equipment	Little gross motor play equipment, in poor repair, or not age appropriate.		Some appropriate gross motor play equipment, but seldom in use (eg inaccessible, requires daily moving, setting up) or little variety of equipment.		Gross motor play equipment is readily available and sturdy; stimulates variety of skills (eg crawling, walking, balancing, climbing). Variety of		Everything in 5, plus equipment is imaginative, flexible, frequently re-arranged by staff and children to maintain and

			extend interest. Several different pieces of equipment at different levels of skill (eg, hammock, tyre swing, knotted rope).	
		equipment on which toddlers can pull up and for them to lift, arrange. Building and dramatic play equipment included in gross motor areas.		
V Time for Gross Motor Activities	No physical activity time outdoors or indoors.	Occasional physical activity time – sporadic.	Regular physical activity time daily, both morning and afternoon.	Regular daily physical activity times with some age-appropriate planned physical activity (eg play with balls, bean bags, follow my leader, obstacle course, skipping, balancing) as well as informal playtime.
VI Adult Attention to Gross Motor Activities	No adult attention provided near gross motor area.	Adult attention to children is minimal (eg adult seated at distance, attention divided with other tasks, several adults chatting, etc). Where supervision is adequate, attention is mainly to safety of children.	Adults discuss with children ideas related to their play, help with resources and build social skills. When appropriate, concepts such as near-far, fast-slow, up-down are related to children's activities. Adults available to lift, carry and swing toddlers.	All as for 5. Also, the children are given scope to learn through movement experience about the environment, themselves and each other in the wide range of safe and stimulating settings which are provided (these include a swimming pond or trampoline). Children are encouraged to think and talk about their own actions and those of others.

III For a rating of 5, space must be adequate for the size of group using it.

7. Social/Emotional Development

	INADEQUATE 1	2	MINIMAL 3	4	GOOD 5	6	EXCELLENT 7
I **Space to be Alone**	No possibility for children to play alone, protected from intrusion by others. Staff consider child being alone undesirable.		Although space is not especially set aside, children are allowed to find space to be alone (eg in play equipment, behind furniture).		Space set aside for one or two children to play, protected from intrusion by others (eg no interruption rule, space out of other children's sight).		Everything in 5, plus play-alone activities provided as part of curriculum, for development of concentration, independence and relaxation.
II **Free Play** **(Free choice)** Child permitted to select materials, companions, and so far as possible, manage play independently.	Either little opportunity for free play or much of day spent in unsupervised free play. Inadequate equipment, toys and games provided for children to use in free play.		Some opportunity for free play, with casual supervision provided as a safety precaution. Free play not seen as an educational opportunity (eg adult misses chance to help child think through solutions to conflicts with others, to encourage child to talk about activity, to introduce concept in relation to child's play).		Ample and varied play equipment, games and toys provided for free play with adult supervision on a regular basis. Free play scheduled regularly each day. Adult involvement is seen as an educational interaction, eg adult helps child to think through social problems, encourages child to talk about activity, introduces concepts in relation to child's play.		As 5, but recognition of the sensitive balance in adult involvement between child's need to explore independently and adult's opportunity to extend learning. New materials/experiences for free play added periodically, in response to children's interests.
III **Group Time** Omit for rooms used exclusively for infants under 9 months of age.	Children kept together as whole group most of the day. Few opportunities for adult to interact with one to three children while other		Some free play available between group activities; however, all planned activities done as a whole group (eg all listen to story, record/tape at the same time).		Planning for small group as well as for large group activities.		Everything in 5 plus different groupings, planned to provide change of pace throughout the day. One-to-one adult-child activities included. Free play and small groups predominate.

	children involved in various free choice activities.			
IV Groupings	Although babies and crawlers are grouped together, otherwise children are assigned to groups where there is a vacancy. Not much significance is attached to consistency of staffing or of peer companionship.	Children are assigned to groups according to their age categories and staff are allocated on the basis of ratios recommended in CA Guidance. Children are moved 'on' when they reach the appropriate age so that the initial group is not always kept together.	Groups are made up of children of approximately the same age or as 'family' group of equivalent size. Regard is paid to continuity of group and of its staff.	Each member of staff is keyworker to 3 babies, 4 toddlers or 8 preschoolers, or to mixed age 'family' of 4-5 children. Each small group contains children of a range of ages within the stage, or in a 'family' group of equivalent size. Regard is paid to continuity of key worker and of group.
V Tone General impression of the quality of interaction.	Staff and children seem strained, voices sound irritable and angry, children cry frequently. Physical contact used principally for control (eg hurrying children along).	Adults inattentive and unresponsive when children are calm and happy but become involved only when problems occur (eg infrequent smiling, loud voices).	Calm but busy atmosphere. Children seem happy most of the time. Staff and children seem relaxed, voices cheerful, frequent smiling. Adults show warmth in physical contact (eg gently holding, hugging). Mutual respect between adults and children and reasonable continuity of adult-child and child-child relationships.	Everything in 5 plus adults prevent problems by careful observation and skilful intervention (eg helping children before minor problems become serious, discussing with children ways of settling conflicts). Curriculum includes planning for development of social skills (eg informally and through stories and discussion groups).
VI Keyworker	No keyworker system.	Keyworker role limited to greeting child/parents and saying goodbye in the evening.	Keyworker role includes having meals with key child, responsible for toileting and overall supervision of	Keyworker role includes responsibility for planning for the needs of the child and family, carrying out

	1	3	5	7
(continued from previous row)			...activities, point of contact for parents.	...assessments, writing reports.
VII Self Esteem	Adults not aware of the importance of self-esteem for optimal development, and often 'put down' children whom they perceive as 'cheeky'.	Adults are aware of the importance of promoting children's self-confidence and do give praise but it is often too general to be meaningful (eg 'What a lovely painting...what a pretty dress', casual passing remarks).	Praise is always realistic and meaningful. Adults consistently take a positive approach, in reminding children of the rules (eg. "We always walk, because..." rather than "Don't run"), in commenting on achievements (eg "You manage so well on the low plank you'll soon be able to balance on the high one") and in enlisting the children's help (eg "Help me to sweep up this sand, a big girl like you will be able to get in all the corners"). Everything possible is done to promote the children's self image. All are encouraged to take responsibility for their own actions, to offer help to those in need and to be reliable in the performance of communal tasks (eg helping to fill the water trough).	All in 5. Also, through close observation of individual strengths adults are able to target accurately their praise and the giving of responsibility. They also work with and through the parents, pointing out those of a child's particular achievements in the facility which can be attributed to home rearing practices.
VIII Opportunities for Children to Care for Others	While children are expected to be sympathetic, this is not facilitated by the staff.	When a child is in trouble, other children are encouraged to offer support and sympathy, but there is no concerted attempt to help children to care effectively for others.	Children are in mixed or 'family' groups. Visits are encouraged by mothers with a new baby. Small pets are kept in appropriate conditions (eg RSPCA recommended) (eg	As 5, plus older children are encouraged to help and play with the younger (eg put on apron, coat). Parents feed, bath, their babies in the playroom. Adults facilitate

	Inadequate	Minimal	Good	Excellent
			hamster, gerbil, guinea pig), for which the children are encouraged to take responsibility (eg bring food, look after). Children are encouraged to feed wild birds in winter. Children take turns to help make the snack.	child-child interaction.
IX Cultural Awareness	No attempt to introduce ethnic or racial diversity eg in dolls, book illustrations or pictures on notice boards. All toys and visible pictures are of one race only.	Some evidence of ethnic and racial diversity in toys and pictorial materials (eg dolls, story books, pictures on notice boards).	Cultural awareness shown by restraint in use of language (perjorative terms avoided etc.) and by liberal inclusion of multiracial and non-sexist materials (eg dolls, story books, pictures on notice boards). Also, sexist, racist, language discouraged.	As 5, plus written policies on multi-culture and gender antidiscrimination; cultural awareness is part of curriculum through planned use of both multi-racial and non-sexist materials (eg holidays of other religions celebrated, cooking of ethnic foods, introduction of a variety of roles for women and men through stories and pictures).
IX Provision for Exceptional Children Exceptional child: any child whose physical, mental or emotional needs are not met by regular programme alone.	No provision or plans for modifying the physical environment or the programme for exceptional children, including gifted. Reluctance to admit children with special needs.	Minor accommodations made to get through the day, but no long-range plans for meeting special needs of exceptional children, including gifted. No attempt to assess degree of need.	Staff assess needs of children and make modifications in environment and integrated programme to meet their special needs. These modifications may require extra resources.	As 5, plus individually planned programme for exceptional children involving parents and using professionally trained person as consultant to guide assessment and planning. Referral to support services, who are invited to work within the facility. Extra resources available (eg an auxiliary, appropriate physical aids).

| Modifications: | Physical environment: | | eg ramps, rest rooms, playground |
| | Programme: | | specialised materials and equipment, use of supportive services, individually planned programme, shorter day, alternative activities. |

II For a 7, find evidence of an educational interaction between children and adults, eg sharing information, questioning to encourage child to speak, helping a child to think through conflicts that result when children choose their play activities.

IX For a 5, non-sexist as well as multi racial materials.

8. Personal Care and Safety Routines

	INADEQUATE 1	2	MINIMAL 3	4	GOOD 5	6	EXCELLENT 7
I Greeting/ Departing Registration	No plans made. Greeting children often neglected. Departure not prepared for. Children often not registered.		Informally understood that someone will greet and register child and will acknowledge departure.		Plans made to ensure warm greeting and organised departure; also registration of all children. Staff member(s) assigned responsibility for greeting and departure of children (eg conversation on arrival; art work and clothes ready for departure).		Everything in 5 plus parents greeted as well as children. Staff use greeting and departure as information-sharing time, to relate warmly to parents.
II Meals/Snacks OR	Meals/snacks of questionable nutritional value served on a haphazard, irregular schedule.		Well-balanced meals/snacks provided in a regular but strict atmosphere, stress on conformity. Meals not used as a pleasant social time and to build self help skills (eg pouring milk, setting table, etc).		Well balanced meals/snacks provided regularly in accordance with a healthy eating policy. Staff member (s) sits with children and provides pleasant physical and social environment during meals. Small group size permits conversation. Variety		Everything in 5 plus interesting physical environment and time planned as a learning experience, including self help skills, talking about children's interests, events of the day, and aspects of foods (colour and where food comes from), promoting healthy

			of meals representing a range of cultures.	eating.
IIa Meals/Snacks (Infants)	Feeding is not timed to children's needs and is of questionable cleanliness and nutritional value.	Clean, nutritionally adequate feeding, on schedule and suited to child's needs.	Clean, nutritionally adequate feeding on schedule suited to child's needs, plus child is held and talked to while bottle fed. Solid food is spoon fed with pleasant adult-child interaction and conversation. Individual attention given.	Everything in 5 plus self-help promoted in feeding (eg. infant-toddler encouraged to finger feed self, then use spoon as ready). Teething materials provided for toddlers who need them; and an adult is on hand to introduce any new tastes/foods.
III Nap/Rest	Nap/rest time or place is inappropriate for children (eg too early or late, rest too short or too long, irregular schedule, crowded area, noisy, poor ventilation. Little or no supervision provided.	Nap/rest is scheduled appropriately with some supervision provided. However, problems exist with supervision, atmosphere or areas used.	Nap/rest is scheduled appropriately with supervision provided. Space is adequate and conducive to resting (eg good ventilation, quiet, comfortable cots/beds placed for privacy, perhaps room darkened). Provision made for early risers and non-nappers.	Everything in 5 plus children helped to relax (eg cuddly toy, soft music, back rubbed, rest begins with favourite song, story).
IV Nappy Changing/ Toileting	Lack of provision interferes with care of children (eg location awkward, no hot water in area, inaccessible to toilets). Sanitary conditions of area not maintained by	Makeshift provision: difficult to keep clean or inaccessible. Not child sized, but sanitary conditions maintained (eg water must be carried to area).	Provisions convenient, well organised, easy to keep clean, even if child sized toilets and sinks not available. Pleasant adult-child interactions. Children are helped to acquire healthy habits (eg wash hands before eating). Adult sensitivity to "accidents".	Everything in 5 plus child sized toilet (potty chairs for toddlers acceptable) and low sinks to promote self-help. Eg: infants: nappy changing used as a time for warm interaction between adult and infant.

V **Personal Care**	staff (eg facilities not clean, staff do not wash hands between children). Little attention paid to personal care (eg hand washing, hair combing).	Inconsistent attention paid to children's care for themselves – hand washing, hair combing, etc, not a regular scheduled part of day's activities.	Scheduled times for personal care eg: tooth brushing with own brush after meals, hands washed before meals and after toileting. Children take a pride in care routines (eg comb hair, put on pinny for water play) which are used to develop positive self concept. Extra clothes to change children or for outdoor play.	Personal care is part of educational programme to promote good health habits. Independence encouraged with proper supervision. Otherwise as 5.
VI **Medicines and First Aid**	Staff attitudes to the administration of medicines unhelpful. No First Aid box nor First Aid manual available.	Medicines, tonics, etc. prescribed at home are casually administered. The establishment has a First Aid box and a simple First Aid manual, not necessarily easily accessible.	Medicines, tonics, etc. are given on the express instructions of the parent/guardian. The child's name and the correct dosage are clearly written on the correct label. A First Aid box, regularly checked, and a simple First Aid manual are readily accessible to the staff. Record made and parent informed of any injury to child occurring in facility.	As 5, plus parent's/guardian's instructions must be in writing. The label giving the child's name and the correct dosage is always read before the dose is administered, always by the same member of staff. Records of dosing are kept. The First Aid box is stored well out of the children's reach.

VII Cleaning Up Routines	Not enough attention is paid to hygiene or orderliness or to training the children in cleaning up. Things are habitually left lying around, and adults may contribute to the sleazy atmosphere by smoking in the playrooms, rest rooms and dining rooms.	Children are encouraged in general to clear up, but are often left to their own devices so that the disorder becomes too great for the children to put to rights on their own, and adults have to take over.	Children are encouraged to clear/clean up after their activities at play, at meals and when engaged in personal care. Adults are on hand to help if the task seems too great for the children alone.	As 5, but adults join in the clearing up tasks and explain the rationale to children, that the equipment should be left as they found it or (if appropriate) in a suitable condition for the next child's turn.
VIII Safety and Accidents	No policy on safety or accidents.	Safety policy is familiar to staff but not written down.	Nursery has written safety policy. All accidents are recorded and report seen by parents.	

II For 5 – social (so group should not be too large) not more than 6 3-4 year olds; 4 2 year olds (at one table)
For 7 – learning experience and social.
V If a scheduled time for personal care consistently followed, rate 5 even if teeth not cleaned.

Appendix 2: Organisations concerned with the day care and education of young children

A directory with full details of nearly 200 national organisations concerned with under fives and their families is available from the National Children's Bureau and VOLCUF, £5.50 to Members, £6.00 to Non-members (plus £3 postage and handling).

Association of Advisers for the Under Fives
Further information: Admin Secretary, 25 Newport Drive, Fishbourne, Chichester PO19 3QQ.
Formed in 1978, the Association aims to provide opportunities for research, information exchange and liaison among professionals concerned with under fives. Has a number of regional groups.

Association of Nursery Training Colleges
Further information: Secretary, R.D. Fullbrook, Chiltern Nursery Training College, 16 Peppard Road, Caversham, Reading RG4 8JZ. (0734 471847)

British Association for Early Childhood Education
Further information: 111 City View House, 463 Bethnal Green Road, London E2 9QY. (071 739 7594)
Encourages the provision of nursery schools and day care, and promotes the interests of young children generally. There are 90 local groups.

Children in Scotland
Further information: Princes House, 5 Shandwick Place, Edinburgh, EH2 4RG. (031 228 8484)
Formed in 1983, based on the Scottish Association of Voluntary Child Care Organisations. Children in Scotland works with voluntary organisations to develop family and child care services on both a national and a local level.

Children in Wales
Further information: 7 Cleeve House, Lambourne Crescent, Cardiff, CF4 5GT. (0222 763 663)

Council For Awards in Children's Care and Education
Further information: 8 Chequer Street, St Albans, Hertfordshire AL1 3AX (0727 847636)

Council for Early Years Awards and the National Nursery Examination Board combined to form CACHE. Deals with enquiries about National Vocational Qualifications in Child Care and Education, and about NNEB qualifications.

Daycare Trust/National Child Care Campaign
Further information: Wesley House, 4 Wild Court, Kingsway, London, WC2B 5AU. (071 405 5617/8)

Founded in 1980, to bring together the many local child care campaigns in the country. Daycare Trust is an information service, NCCC aims to promote child care issues nationally and locally and to ensure equal opportunities.

Equality Learning Centre
Further information: London Voluntary Resource Centre, 356 Holloway Road, London N7 6PA (071 700 8127)

Maternity Alliance
Further information: Sue Hunt, 15 Britannia Street, London WC1X 9JP. (071 837 1265)

Campaigns for improvements in the health care, social and financial support and legal rights of mothers, fathers and babies.

National Association for Maternal and Child Welfare
Further information: 40-42 Osnaburgh Street, London NW1 3ND. (071 383 4117)

Furtherance of education in maternal and child welfare, and promotion of research. Examination structure in Family Life, Child Care and Human Development. Holds conferences. Has a range of publications.

National Association of NNEB Tutors
Further information: Secretary, Clare Wade, 31 Carleton Avenue, Fulwood, Preston PR2 6YA.

National Association of Nursery and Family Care
Further information: C. Dallimore, 12 Conyers Avenue, Birkdale, Southport PR8 4SZ.

Formerly the National Association of Nursery Matrons.

National Association of Nursery Nurses
Further information: Phyllis Mitchell, 10 Meriden Court, Gt Clacton, Essex CO15 4XH. (0255 476707)

National Campaign for Nursery Education
Further information: BLM, Box 6216, London WC1N 3XX
Works to increase nursery provision by local authorities by public campaigning. Has local branches.

National Child Care Campaign *see* **Daycare Trust**

National Council of Voluntary Child Care Organisations (Childcare)
Further information: Childcare, Unit 4, Pride Court, 80/82 White Lion Street, London N1 9PF. (071 833 3319)
Established in 1942, NCVCCO is a grouping of more than 70 voluntary child care organisations which work with children, young people and families in response to social needs. NCVCCO administers the allocation of money from the DHSS Small Grants Scheme to local projects.

National Play Information Centre
Further information: Linda Antell, Information Officer, 359/361 Euston Road, London NW1 3AL. (071 388 1277)
National body, established in 1988, to promote interests and ensure that play is recognised as a vital component of childhood.

National Private Day Nurseries Association
Further information: 21 Kirklees Close, Farsley, Pudsey, Leeds LS28 5TE (0532 550752)

Organisation Mondiale Pour L'education Prescholaire (OMEP)
Further information: A. Lewis, OMEP (UK) Secretary, 144 Eltham Road, London SE9 5LW. (081 850 3981)
Founded after a World Conference in 1948, OMEP aims to promote a greater understanding of children under the age of eight years, and to share the experiences of different countries.

Parents at Work
Further information: 77 Holloway Road, London N7 8JZ. (071 700 5771)
Formerly called Working Mothers Association. A network of support groups for working parents, for the exchange of information and experiences. Formed in 1985. Seeks to establish "good practice" guidelines for day care of young children.

Playmatters/National Toy Libraries Association

Further information: 68 Churchway, London, NW1 1LT. (071 387 9592)

National body for the many toy libraries in the country. They operate as a preventive service, filling gaps in the existing provision for all families with babies and young children, and people with special needs.

Thomas Coram Research Unit

Further information: 27-28 Woburn Square, London, WC1H 0AA. (071 612 6957)

Undertakes policy orientated research concerned with the family, with the education and development of children, and with the services provided for children and their families.

UK Central Council for Nursing, Midwifery & Health Visiting

Further information: 23 Portland Place, London, W1N 3AF. (071 637 7181)

The UKCC is the statutory body responsible for registration, professional conduct, and the education and training policy for all members of the profession in the UK.

Voluntary Organisations' Liaison Council for the Under Fives (VOLCUF)

Further information: 77 Holloway Road, London N7 8JZ. (071 607 9573)

Formed in 1976 as a federation for many different voluntary and other organisations concerned with under fives and their families, and as a forum for the development and dissemination of ideas.

Working for Childcare (formerly Workplace Nurseries Campaign)

Further information: 77 Holloway Road, London N7 8JZ. (071 700 0281)

The campaign for quality child care for working parents.

Index

The index covers the Foreword and Chapters 1–9. It does not include the Bibliography and Appendices. Entries are arranged in letter-by-letter order (hyphens and spaces between words are ignored.) Page references for figures and tables are shown in italic, eg *60*.